The Frustrated Leader

Using Frustration To Accomplish Your Vision

ADVICE FOR THE CHRISTIAN LEADER

by
MYRON EDMONDS, D.MIN

Copyright © 2019 by MyRon Edmonds

All rights reserved. No part of this publication may be reproduced, distributed, or transmitted in any form or by any means, including photocopying, recording, or other electronic or mechanical methods, without the prior written permission of the publisher, except in the case of brief quotations embodied in critical reviews and certain other noncommercial uses permitted by copyright law. For permission requests, write to the publisher, addressed ¡°Attention: Permissions Coordinator," at the address below.

MyRon Edmonds
www.myronedmonds.com

Ordering Information:
Quantity sales. Special discounts are available on quantity purchases by corporations, associations, and others. For details, contact the publisher at the address above.
Orders by U.S. trade bookstores and wholesalers.

Please contact MyRon Edmonds:
email: bookmyrone@gmail.com
Facebook: https://www.facebook.com/myron.edmonds
Instagram: instagram.com/itsmyronlive
Twitter: https://twitter.com/itsMyRonlive

Developed and Edited by Sharee Moore Dynasty Publishers

Also edited by Paul Nixon for Virtual V.P.

The Frustrated Leader

Using Frustration To Accomplish Your Vision

ADVICE FOR THE CHRISTIAN LEADER

by
MYRON EDMONDS, D.MIN
www.myronedmonds.com

From MyRon:
To my wife Shaneé,
daughter Teylor,
son Camden

Table of Contents

Acknowledgements viii

Foreward ix

Introduction xi

Chapter 1   The Frustrated Visionary Leader 1

Chapter 2   The Psychology of Frustration:
            Lessons from Fortnite and
            Candy Crush 17

Chapter 3   The 7 Sources of Frustration 29

Chapter 4   The System: Lessons from a
            Football Team and Sandwich War 43

Chapter 5   7 Key Questions 55

Chapter 6   The Theology of Frustration:
            You're in Good Company 69

Chapter 7   Focus: A Lesson from a Bad Piano 86

Notes 94

About the Author 98

PRAISE FOR
THE FRUSTRATED LEADER

"Dr. MyRon Edmonds focuses on the angst that drives one in ministry and shares insight through his personal journey. As he unpacks the subject of "frustration" you will experience many "aha moments" to fuel your leadership. Get this! Read this! It will encourage you in the journey of ministry."
—Ivan L. Williams, Sr., *Director-North American Division Ministerial Association*

"Who knew that frustration could be God's gateway to leadership greatness? Who knew that frustration could be God's "check engine light" to pry us off of our puny agendas onto His supernatural plans? Thank you Dr. MyRon Edmonds for reminding us that God's gifts can come in strange packages!" "The Frustrated Leader" Three words. Get-The-Book!!
—Dr. Jesse Wilson, *Professor Oakwood University*

"The Frustrated Leader surprisingly adjusts your negative response to leadership challenges into an honest appreciation of frustration in leadership that ultimately brings about a positive change. Frustration is foundational to leadership; This book affirms it."
—Vandeon D. Griffin, Assoc. *Director of Youth Ministries, North American Division*

"One emotion that every leader at any level will face is frustration. Many times, we look at it as evidence to give up and turn back. In this book, MyRon totally reframes that and challenges us to use the frustrations we experience as fuel for even more effective leadership. Don't read this book alone. Take your entire team through it."
　—Kymone Hinds, Creativity Consultant, Ideas to Life, LLC

"The Frustrated Leader not only captures the struggle every visionary leader experiences as they're leading change, but it provides practical solutions for navigating around these struggles. A must read for every leader!"
　—Seth Yelorda, CEO Bridge Solutions, LLC

"Are you frustrated? Leading people would be awesome if it weren't for the people. Wherever people are involved, frustration ensues. Dr. Edmonds tackles this subject in a way only he can. Get this book!"
　—Roger Hernandez, Ministerial and Evangelism Director, Southern Union Conference of Seventh-Day Adventists

Acknowledgments

I would like to thank my wife Shaneé for being my number one cheerleader and supporter. I love you so much for being my rock. I love you to the moon and back.

To my amazing children Teylor and Camden for being awesome kids and great leaders themselves. Can't wait to see where God takes you both. Love you guys.

To my Dad and Mom, you guys have taught me everything I know of what it means to be a leader. Much of the substance of this book was caught and taught from you. I love you and thank you.

To my amazing associate pastors Regina Johnson and Kimberly Bulgin, iron sharpens iron and because of you I am a better leader. Love you both.

To all my friends on the "Code Red" text thread. Thanks for challenging me through every text to be a better leader.

To all my brothers on the "Too Real" text thread. You know who you are. Words cannot express how much you guys have helped me in the formation of my thinking about leadership and this book. Much love to you all.

Finally, I praise you Holy Spirit for your guidance and patience with me during my times of frustration.

Foreword

Given what I do, I'm constantly inundated with leadership books all angling to spellbind with the latest nuance on how to think about leadership. Rarely have I found a book that doesn't teach me at least something, if it is only patience. But every now and again, there comes along a book that tackles a subject matter in such a totally unexpected way, that you have to push the pause button, gather yourself, for you know intuitively that this will not be a speed-read. It's the kind of book that represents an inflection point in the sense that the announced subject taps into something deep within, which had never been given voice to.

That's how I felt, when at 36,000 feet in the air, I started to read the final draft of Dr. MyRon Edmond's latest book. It's not so much that his work breaks new ground by expounding on some novel leadership theory; it's more personal than that. Right out of the gate the book forces you into an uncomfortable space—places you would prefer to "leave it be." Why dredge it up? That disturbing feeling that every leader knows all too well: frustration! Only a few books have had this visceral effect on me. This is one of them.

It's axiomatic that most leaders have known both the exhilaration of daring greatly, and that sinking feeling of being blocked and stymied on all sides. The leader is clear on the vision yet frustrated on the execution.

The author, on a guttural level, compels leaders to say it out loud: "God, where are you in all of this?" Where are you in the tossing and turning of those sleepless nights?

I most often experienced the painful pits of frustration in the aftermath of those interminable meetings when a well-meaning (or not so well-meaning) board member would torpedo the very thing that could move the organization forward, and then weeks later, declare sanctimoniously, "Our organization feels rudderless—we're not moving." I knew while sitting in the room that I was headed for a sleepless night of wandering a darkened house crying, calling on God, and sometimes just wanting to curse. More often, I was wanting to quit.

Those of us who lead quit all the time—often on a weekly basis. It's one of the occupational hazards of leadership. And frustration is a key driver.

So, is it possible for a leader to use frustration to his/her benefit?

The winsome aspect of this book is that MyRon speaks poignantly as a fellow traveler—one who grapples with being a frustrated leader. He refuses to off-load pop- cultured wisdom - with its quick fixes - to the waiting masses. Instead, he leads the reader on a growth journey that is at first confrontative and then it provides a release.

MyRon's notion of frustration as part of the creative process of leading represents a mind shift. But without this shift, leaders can end up being frustrated about being frustrated.

The fact is, no leader "worth the salt in their bread" gets a pass, especially if they are intent on leading well. This book is all about leaders learning how to not shrink from the crippling feeling of frustration, but to lean into it as a normal, albeit uncomfortable, step toward embracing the full range of possibilities that God reserves uniquely for leaders— frustrated leaders.

Fredrick Russell
PRINCIPAL, TRUE NORTH LEADERSHIP GROUP

Introduction

The purpose of this book is to help you use frustration as leverage for accomplishing great things. We need a healthy dosage of frustration to keep us pursuing success and we need to eliminate unhealthy doses of frustration that paralyze us into a long-term negative mindset, or apathy. I strongly warn you against allowing your frustration to run free. You have to put a harness and bridle on your frustration before taking it for a ride. Ultimately, I'm hoping to give you practical tools for doing just that.

In his bestselling book *E-Myth*, Michael E. Gerber, one of the global leaders in transformational business coaching, suggests that there are three ways people usually perceive organizational frustrations:

1. Self-Directed
- "I am the cause of my own frustration."
- "I don't have enough time to do what I need to do."
- "I'm not good enough to lead these people."
- "I'm burned out and don't have any energy to make a difference."

2. Outer-Directed
- "You are the cause of my frustration."
- "I need more team members."
- "Our organization is broke. We don't have money to do anything."
- "These volunteers are lazy and lack commitment."

3. System-Directed
- "The lack of an effective system is the cause."
- "Our vision is not clear and compelling."
- "We have a culture of criticism."
- "Our parent organization is not supportive."

So, all frustrations don't have the same origin, but accurately identifying what kind of frustration you're dealing with is critical to leveraging its power to ignite a solution-driven vision. We will revisit these three frustrations later in the book.

My definition for leadership frustration is this— frustration is nothing more than an indicator that something in you, your organization or ministry needs attention. Critical to dealing with frustration is the ability to pinpoint exactly where the frustration is coming from so we can effectively fix whatever is broken. Most of us who own cars have experienced this when that annoying bright yellow "check engine" light comes on. Annoying as it may be, the purpose of that light is to alert you that something is wrong. In most cases, you have to get the light turned off in order to register your car. I've personally been guilty of simply trying to jimmy the light off, without addressing the issue with the car, in order to avoid spending lots of money. I was treating the light as if it were the problem when the check engine light was designed to direct me to look for the problem. That's how frustration works. Frustration is not the problem. Frustration is the "check engine" light in your organization or ministry to analyze what the problem is that's hindering progress and ultimately the accomplishment of your vision. Strong and intuitive leaders don't allow frustration to frustrate them neither do they avoid the pain of frustration by sweeping it under the carpet. They recognize that frustration is a signal that indicates we need to think critically about the underlying causes of our frustration. They see frustration as blessing not a curse.

My hope is that this book will help transform your perspective regarding your frustrations and leverage your frustration to accomplish your vision. Because:

Frustrated people care.
Frustrated people are visionaries.
Frustrated people innovate.
Frustrated people solve problems.
Frustrated people frustrate the status quo.
Frustrated people change the world.

Let's get started.

CHAPTER 1

The Frustrated Visionary Leader

"The feeling of frustration forces some to seek inspiration."
— Sara Wellington

I am a pastor. Which means I deal with church people. Which means I'm always in a constant state of agonizing frustration. Which means I don't get paid enough for the amount of frustration that I feel. Okay, I'm just kidding. I love pastoring and I love church people (at least today). But leading in ministry is the most frustrating experience I have ever had in my life. I can't tell you how many times I've quit only to delete my resignation letter and jump back in again. The amount of stress produced in me because of my frustration has caused hair loss, depression, loss of sleep, fluctuating weight, fits of rage, confusion and regular appointments with the therapist. I remember when I first started pastoring. I was the epitome of naïveté. I had a big vision to change my church, the entire city and win thousands to Christ, all in less than 6 months, just as I had read in the book of Acts. Although God moved in a moment in Acts 2, I wanted to be more realistic by adding 6 months. Calling myself naive is an understatement. As soon as I began my ministry, my vision turned into a nightmare when I realized I had an overwhelming amount of problems to deal with, which seemed to be blocking my success. I had money problems. Non-stop people problems. Administrative problems. Community problems. Internal problems. External problems. Problems. Problems. Problems.

If you were to talk to me during that season of my ministry all you would have heard from me was how many problems I had. I complained constantly. Whined incessantly. Bellyached continually about my life in ministry. I had become so negative and cynical, that my frustration became my drug. It came out in how I treated my members. It affected my preaching and teaching. My chronic frustration even affected my marriage and family life because I couldn't turn off my negative mindset.

Many of you can relate to this. You had so much optimism, but as soon as you started serving in ministry your tune of great expectations turned into the blues. What I didn't realize was that my frustrations were not the problem. My problem was my attitude towards frustration. I see this in so many leaders, especially in the church. They have bad attitudes that limit their ability to see a God-sized vision. They don't realize that the most valuable asset they have to accomplish much for God is their belief and attitude. It is my strong opinion that a bad attitude in a leader is equivalent to immorality. It's leadership malpractice. Leaders are thermostats not thermometers. A thermostat sets the temperature, while a thermometer reflects the temperature. Are you setting the temperature or reflecting it?

It is my belief that one of Satan's most tried and true attacks against spiritual leaders is attacking their perspective and attitude. If he can cause you to lose faith and sap you of your passion and drive, everything else he wants to do will be easy. Our mindset is everything. The old adage says, "Your attitude often determines your altitude." What I learned has become a consuming passion, which is, the very thing you are frustrated about contains in it the raw materials to accomplish your vision. I'm not trying to sell you some pie-in-the sky positive thinking pep talk. I'm sharing with you the secret that most transformational leaders know and understand—frustration is power. I'm here to challenge what you believe about frustration and hope that by the last page, you'll realize that it's actually good for you.

My experience as a leader has taught me that people who aren't passionate about what they do are generally unbothered and at peace experiencing little to no frustration. Your passion and frustration are intricately connected. Un-frustrated people are boring and make very little impact in this world. This book isn't for those people. This book is for YOU – visionary leaders who are passionate and driven to bring about change. Leaders who experience frustration almost as your normal. Your vision and passion actually create the space where frustration brews. I have found that no matter where or whom you lead, or how passionate you are about leading, if you *really* love what you're doing you *will* experience frustration. Here's why.

Leaders who are passionate and who have a huge vision and mission to accomplish are rarely" satisfied with themselves, their organization, followers or current situation. They're just not! They stay hungry and hopeful for things to be better. They despise mediocrity and they are enemies to the status quo. So, is being frustrated really such a bad thing? Perhaps it's time to look at it differently. Learn to see your frustration as visionary leadership energy. See it as one of many signs that you simply care about what you're doing.

Deep caring and the frustration that follows are often the starting point of either failure or success. The secret is in inviting *balance* to have a seat at the table. If you're *not* frustrated there's something wrong. If you're *too* frustrated there's also something wrong.

The Frustrated Visionary Leader

Visionary leaders are frustrated leaders. They always see a better way, a preferred future, change or improvement. History is cluttered with leaders who have accomplished great things but there are few who have changed the world. The leaders that change the world are what I call visionary leaders. There's not enough space in this book to talk about each of them, but there is one person that universally is revered as a visionary leader: The Rev. Dr. Martin Luther King, Jr.

Dr. King helped inspire the Civil Rights Movement that became the moral conscience of a nation in a time when it was lawful to oppress people of color. But what is not often appreciated is the inner turmoil and pain that King experienced in wanting more for his people. He was truly a frustrated leader.

Yet he had a vision. A dream. He is known for his "dream." Yet what is often overlooked is that this dream was fueled by an inner pain and dissatisfaction about racial inequality. Seeing Black people being treated as second class citizens made him angry. NPR.com did a series of articles on "The Other Side of

Anger." There was one article dedicated to King entitled, "The Power of Martin Luther King Jr.'s Anger." The article reflects:

> "When Martin Luther King, Jr. was in high school, he won an oratorical contest sponsored by the Negro Elks. He and a beloved teacher were returning home in triumph, riding on a bus, when some white passengers got on. The white bus driver ordered King and his teacher to give up their seats and cursed them. King wanted to stay seated, but his teacher urged him to obey the law. They had to stand in the aisle for the 90 miles back to Atlanta, Ga.
>
> 'That night will never leave my memory,' King told an interviewer, decades later. 'It was the angriest I have ever been in my life.'_ King turned his frustration and anger into a dream and a vision.
>
> As he grew older, and went to college and theological school, Martin Luther King, Jr. realized that non-violent resistance offered a way to channel anger into positive forms of protest. 'If you internalize anger, and you don't find a channel, it can destroy you,' [said Bernice King]. 'That's why when Daddy reiterated, 'Hate is too great a burden to bear,' he knew it was corrosive and erosive.'"[1]

King's experience with frustration and anger is the experience of most visionary leaders. They are generally upset about something.

Called to Frustration

Being frustrated and bothered by something is the fuel that makes the visionary leader's engine run. As a visionary, you see the problem and the solution, and you are burdened to take action. The burden then morphs into an internal frustration, because every desire to improve or change something often faces an equal resistance or complacency towards change. It is because you are a visionary that you often see it first and feel the pain of it more intensely than others. You lose sleep at night over it. It's hard to focus on anything else except the frustration. You feel alone and misunderstood. Sometimes you may even ask yourself, "Am I out of my mind?" But this state of frustration is God-given.

There are some special ones that God has chosen to disturb and upset. If you're reading this book, more than likely, you are one of them. God doesn't frustrate you because He takes pleasure in seeing you stressed. He frustrates you because He wants you to do something about it!

Learn to see your frustration as an asset. It is your call to action, not permission to slip into negativity or to become an overly critical person. From this space, frustration will inspire you, not depress you.

Visionary Leaders Gut Check

Yes, you've been appointed and positioned by God to embrace this holy frustration. But I have to be honest with you about being *called* to frustration. Human nature is hostile towards vision, because vision is about change, and change makes us uncomfortable. So, don't think that being a visionary is the road of least resistance. Prepare your mind for a fight. There are at least three frustrating fights that you need to prepare yourself for as a visionary leader.

Fight with the Frustration from Without

Anytime you seek to improve, transform or provide a solution to a situation you will experience frustration from external resistance. This could be people, systems, mindsets, lack of resources, or even spiritual attacks that obstruct progress. External fights that cause frustration are the most conspicuous. These fights arise because your vision is a threat to the status quo.

For example, maybe you are a youth leader who is frustrated because young people are leaving the church. Your solution is to shift the worship services to be more youth friendly and to involve young people in the overall decision making of the church. When you raise this issue with church leadership, you are met with resistance. Leadership would rather keep the older members happy and comfortable than open themselves to new methods. So, they seek to block your ideas and suggestions in meetings.

This is what a frustrating external fight looks like. It generally comes from the ones who stand to benefit the most by your vision for change. This is exactly what Moses experienced when he was trying to get the Israelites into the promised land. They resisted him even though it would benefit them to leave bondage and go to freedom. One of the most difficult things to bear when dealing with the *frustration from without* is being misunderstood. As I'm writing this, many of you feel this on a very personal level. You have the most sincere intentions, yet people question your motives, integrity, and sincerity, leaving you feeling alone and even rejected. Why? Because your vision for change is a threat to their comfort and identity. I heard someone say that "people aren't resistant to change as much as they are resistant to loss." If change will threaten them losing their position, power and personal comfort then they will interpret you as a foe not a friend.

Fight with the Frustration from Within

Then there is the *fight with frustration from within*. This represents the internal struggle and fight you have with yourself, which results in frustration. It is manifested in your own mind. This is the most inconspicuous of all our fights with frustration because it's easier to see the external sources of frustration coming from others than the internal fights that limit our success.

As leaders, our reflex when dealing with resistance is to immediately blame the external sources rather than look at ourselves and consider what role we play in fueling our frustration. Many times, our number one source of frustration is hidden within our own psyche. We see it when dealing with our own self-defeating thoughts and insecurities that question our abilities, our spirituality, and even our sanity. This is definitely the least obvious fight because it requires soul searching, self-awareness and admitting that we are a part of the problem.

When I first started in ministry, my initial reaction to my frustration was to blame others. I would say things like "these people have no vision," "they're clueless," "they're difficult," "they're stubborn," "they don't trust me," "they don't love Jesus," or even "these folks are demonic and evil." The truth is, some of this, if not all of it, *could* be true, but this mindset only allows us to see others as a part of the problem. Let me remind you of something: you were called by God to change what you are complaining about. That's why you're the one with the vision. But also recognize that the vision God gave you is not just about *them*. It's also about *you*.

Vision not only changes the situation and solves the problem; it also grows and matures the leader. Let me be transparent with you. One of my struggles, as a person and a leader, is my desire to be well thought of and liked. A lot of leaders struggle with this. This approval addiction is a weakness in my character that often has me interpreting resistance as a personal attack. The truth is, it's not them. It's my own internal issues and struggles with whether I'm good enough. With this kind of baggage, it's easy for me to care too much about what people think and say about me.

Many of you reading this need to do some serious introspection. Our internal issues become the lens though which we see our frustrations. This is especially true of how we view people who resist our vision. We must not demonize everyone that doesn't see things our way. We do not want to take things so personal. Leaders that possess self-awareness about their own issues and growth areas realize it's not always someone else's fault. They're not only tough critics on others but they are equally, if not more so, willing to apply a healthy dose of criticism on themselves.

Fight with the Frustration from Above

Of the three fights, none is more beneficial and simultaneously stressful than the frustration fight we have from *above*. Have you ever had to fight frustration with God? I know for me, I have these conversations with God asking Him a bunch of "why" questions:

- Why did you give me this vision?
- Why did you bring me here?
- Why won't you answer me?
- Why are you letting them hold up progress?
- Why won't you just give me the money?
- Why are you taking so long?
- Why aren't you speaking to me?
- Why won't you just destroy all my enemies? (LOL! Ok, just kidding!)

How frustrating is that? Having to deal with a God that seems to be holding up His own plan for you. You and I both know that at the snap of a finger God could remove all your frustrations but many times He won't. Especially when you are expending so much spiritual energy praying and fasting and obeying; but He's not moving fast enough or in the way you need Him to move. THIS is frustrating.

As we seek to deal with our frustrations, we have to be honest and deal with God as a part of our frustration. There is nothing spiritually wrong with being frustrated with God. He can handle your frustrations. Many of us, in the name of "keeping it real," will go off on someone and give them a piece of our mind because of our frustration. How many of you have given God a piece of your mind? Don't worry it's biblical (and quite therapeutic). King David understood this and exemplified this in Psalm 13:1-4 when he cried out in frustration:

The Frustrated Visionary Leader

"How long, Lord? Will you forget me forever?
How long will you hide your face from me?
How long must I wrestle with my thoughts
and day after day have sorrow in my heart?
How long will my enemy triumph over me?
Look on me and answer, Lord my God.
Give light to my eyes, or I will sleep in death,
and my enemy will say, "I have overcome him,"
and my foes will rejoice when I fall."[2]

Did you feel the passion and frustration? He almost sounded a little disrespectful telling God to "Look on me and answer!" David was a visionary leader and visionary leaders are honest with God and don't hold back their frustration from Him. This kind of honesty with God doesn't hurt the leader but helps the leader deal with their frustration. The old hymn says, "Oh what peace we often forfeit. Oh what needless pain we bear. All because we do not carry, everything to God in prayer." I really believe we should take everything to God in prayer, not just our good and clean thoughts. We need to take all of our feelings, emotions and frustrations to God.

I've learned that God is more interested in what He's doing IN you than what He's doing THROUGH you. We often develop tunnel vision while accomplishing the vision and have the tendency to forget that God is working ON us as well.

Essentially, the process of being frustrated with God is about deepening our relationship with Him. If God instantaneously removes our frustrations, there are things about Him we would never see. Feeling frustrated with God does one thing, which is critical in coping with the frustration—it helps you develop an honest prayer life. Frustration with God removes all religious pretense and formality in our interaction with Him. It gets you to a place where you are 100% authentic with God. You come to Him as, Abba, your father, rather than judge and ruler. He sees your plans, petitions, your feelings, desires, moods, fears, issues, and insecurities. When you enter this fight with God, like Jacob, you come into the fight strong and confident. After the fight, you leave wounded, but dependent on Him without a trace of fear for any man.

Let's Fight!

I'm calling you up and out of stagnation to stand firm in your appointment. Don't take pushback personally. If you can understand this, you will operate in a renewed sense of purpose and steadfastness. As a visionary leader, you sort of have a sixth sense to see what needs changing. But you also have a propensity to feel frustration. Small stuff frustrates you. Big stuff frustrates you. People FRUSTRATE you. Situations FRUSTRATE you. Delays FRUSTRATE you. Why? Because *change* is exactly what *you* have been appointed to do! That fire in you is there so that you can stimulate, facilitate, and instigate change! You are a bonafide change agent. A way maker. A mover and shaker.

If you are called to create change, yet you don't get upset (a.k.a. FRUSTRATED) when people and situations resist change — you can breathe a deep sigh of relief because you do not carry the mantle of a true visionary. I said it and you can fight me on it. Frustration comes with the territory. It's in you, and there's no getting around it.

My Story

Let me tell you a story about how I became a frustrated visionary leader.

I am the only biological child out of five. Our family has three boys and two girls. My parents adopted my other siblings. Each one of my adopted brothers and sisters who came to live with us during my childhood had experienced extreme cases of childhood trauma including physical, sexual and emotional abuse. In addition to the abuse they experienced in their biological families, they also experienced extreme poverty and violence that is so common to those growing up in the inner city. Despite all of their difficult experiences, all except one has attended and/or graduated from college. They earn a good living, and are currently raising families of their own, in much better circumstances. I attribute their success, in a large part, to the change of environment they experienced when they moved in and became family.

A loving family that has structure, an emphasis on achievement, spirituality and compassionate discipline has turned their lives around. Observing and participating in this process has given me a burden - an inner frustration - to help children and families from inner cities to live successful lives. I want to create communities that help inspire people to reach their full potential - just like my brothers and sisters did.

There are a couple of things that burn me up about this. First, the factors that made their lives so much more difficult than other folks' frustrate me. It just seems unfair that whole populations of people are marginalized and limited from success because of their skin color or their neighborhood. It bothers me that there are many black and brown children that are systemically limited in achieving their dreams. They are going hungry every day. They are experiencing trauma. They are going to subpar schools that serve as prison pipelines. It angers me that monies flow through local governments, and even churches, yet those dollars do not reach the fatherless and the disenfranchised youth of our society. I'm getting riled up even as I'm typing this! I personally feel a moral compulsion to base my ministry around helping the poor and underprivileged of our society. I lose sleep at night over this.

The second thing that burns me up about this is the fact that many of our churches seem oblivious and apathetic to the needs of this population of people. The Bible is replete with admonitions to care for the fatherless, widows and the poor. Yet many churches are fighting over carpet colors, worship styles, generational power struggles and theological issues, instead of fighting for "the least of these" who cannot fight for themselves. That sickens me! Jesus based His whole ministry around "proclaiming good news to the poor ... proclaiming freedom to prisoners ... and setting the oppressed free." Despite this, many Christians are dressing up in their church clothes, packing out their elaborate buildings once a week, while making absolutely no impact on their communities. If these so-called "churches" disappeared, their neighborhoods would not miss them. The church has been empowered and called to do so much more!

This frustrates the heck out of me!

Because I feel so passionately frustrated about this (I hope you can feel my fire through the pages), it is an indicator that God has called me to do something about it. God doesn't waste holy frustration on anybody. Your frustration is your anointing. Your frustration is your calling. Answer it.

Dig Deeper

The reason I'm sharing this is because I want you to understand that your experiences in life often drive your frustrations.

As you are learning to manage frustration, you must also investigate the origins of your frustration. Do a personal assessment of your feelings. Ask a bunch of "why" questions so that you can clearly see the underlying trigger. Understanding the origin and motivation of your frustration will help you understand yourself better. As you become more self-aware about your frustration, you will be better equipped to use frustration rather than being used by it. It's also important to recognize that everyone will not share the same frustrations. You shouldn't be frustrated about *everything*. Some of the things that mess with me are things that don't mess with you. So, it's critical that you identify your own frustration and don't simply adopt someone else's. Identifying the "why" of your frustration helps you navigate it, deal with it and leverage it.

Summary Points
- Visionary leaders tend to see problems and solutions first.
- Visionary leaders feel the pain of frustration more intensely than others.
- Visionary leaders sometimes question themselves.
- Frustration is God-given.
- Frustration is an asset because it's a call-to-action.
- Frustration is a product of our unique life experiences.
- Frustration creates a fight without, within and above.

Questions for Reflection
- What frustrates you and motivates you to want to take action?
- Why are you frustrated about this? Ask more "why" questions! Go deeper still.

The Frustrated Leader

- What is your story? Is there any connection between your life's experiences and your leadership frustration?
- What can be done about this frustration? What else?

CHAPTER 2

The Psychology of Frustration: Lessons from Fortnite and Candy Crush

"If we stay frustrated and angry with no action behind it, we get our bodies and brains used to that being our baseline, and it decreases our ability to experience joy and satisfaction."
— Dr. DaNella Knight

I need to warn you. This is probably the most important chapter in this book so far. The information in this chapter is what separates those who are motivated by frustration and those who are paralyzed by it.

Frustration is a complex subject. I don't want our handling of this topic to be oversimplified, even in the context of visionary leadership. Frustration is neurological. It happens in our minds, therefore it's also psychological. Because of this, let's go deeper to see exactly what is happening when we feel frustrated.

First, let's clarify something. Prolonged stress, anger and constant feelings of frustration aren't good for you. There are numerous studies about the detrimental effects prolonged stress has on your health. Toxic stress elevates the risks for heart disease, negatively impacts the immune system, and causes depression. Constant frustration can make you sick, yet it has a purpose.

"Frustration moves us into action, gets us into higher alertness so we can act decisively about varied situations," says clinical psychologist Dr. DaNella Knight. "If we stay frustrated and angry with no action behind it, we get our bodies and brains used to that being our baseline, and it decreases our ability to experience joy and satisfaction," Knight explains.[1]

Like all emotions, frustration triggers the "fight or flight" survival response in our limbic system. This is a response that helps us take action. It gives us the strength we need to defend ourselves or run from whatever challenge or obstacle presents itself. When frustration fails to fill a constructive framework, that's when you've got problems. Without a response, action, or movement, frustration serves no purpose! I've seen many leaders wallow in frustration. They cuddle with it. Frustration becomes their identity rather than their motivation. No sir!

Fortunately, history has great examples of men and women who were catapulted into greatness because of their frustrations. Moses was frustrated with Egyptian abuse, Jesus was frustrated with religion, Mother Teresa was frustrated with selfishness, Nelson Mandela was frustrated with apartheid and Martin Luther King, Jr. was frustrated with racism. The reason they are great visionary leaders is because they listened to those frustrations and flipped them into transformative solutions. They didn't waste their energy in complaining and complacency. What are you frustrated about? What gets you mad? Whatever cause frustrates you the most is probably the one you were born to change.

What is frustration?

Frustration comes from the Latin word *frustrare* which means "disappoint." Frustration is a feeling of disappointment, discouragement, anger or annoyance as a result of the unmet expectations of something deemed important to you. The components of frustration are expectations and obstacles. You become frustrated when you expect something to happen, but it doesn't due to some kind of obstacle. For example, I'm driving home. My expectation is to get home in 15 minutes, but there is bumper-to-bumper traffic. I'm now frustrated. I had an expectation and an obstacle has hindered it from being met.

The Frustration Cycle

The Frustration Cycle begins with an unmet expectation, followed by feelings of frustration. Next, there is either a constructive response or a destructive response. A constructive response leads to a resolution of the problem. A destructive response leads back to increased feelings of frustration.

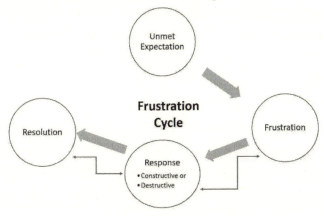

The way to break this cycle is by changing our response. Our response is based on whether or not we believe the source of frustration can be resolved. Belief is everything! In scientific nomenclature, this is called the science of hope, and *belief* is called resilience. If there is anyone who should exhibit resilience it is a visionary leader.

Types of Leaders

The past 20 years of leadership experiences have taught me that there are basically two kinds of leaders: those who are paralyzed by frustrations and those who are pushed by them. Those paralyzed by frustrations fall into three categories:

1. The Chronic Complainer
2. The Coward
3. The Self-Conscious

The Chronic Complainer
This leader is paralyzed by the problems. They are usually an excessive talker as well. They are glass-half-empty leaders whose negative outlooks make their way to their mouths. These people literally talk themselves out of any possible solutions. The danger with this group is that they call themselves being "realistic" and they condescendingly look down on anyone that doesn't buy into their dark way of thinking. They are hostile to anyone who chooses to focus on solutions because it exposes *their* own cynicism. Their words and attitude are contagious. As a leader, you need to guard your mouth from negative speaking. I'm not against being honest about situations, but excessive

and chronic negative-speak, and focusing on problems renders leaders useless.

The Coward

This one is a leader who is paralyzed by fear. They are afraid of failure, of others, of success or anything that will require courage or taking a stand. Frustration has a way of making itself bigger in your imagination than it really is. Cowardly leaders interpret their own personal fears as a reason to not seek resolution. The truth is, fear often serves as a moment of growth for a leader. It's a call to move out of one's comfort zone. A comfortable, safe leader who is afraid of everything and everyone cannot lead people of faith and belief. They can only produce more cowards. Just as complaining is contagious, so is cowardice. Acting courageously is not moving without legitimate fears, it's moving in the face of those fears.

The Self-Conscious

This type is paralyzed by their own personal interests. Many times, these leaders are internally frustrated because things didn't go their way. These leaders will only move out of their frustration if it benefits them personally. These self-serving leaders are often in frustration because they can't handle what leadership is really all about. It's about the team versus the individual. Their personal insecurities rise up often, especially when they are not the center of attention or receiving the credit. They appear to be making moves, but I put them in the paralysis category because they are making moves *without others*. Their selfish ambition creates frustration in them and in others who can see their blaring insecurities.

Called Leaders

The kind of leaders that are pushed and not paralyzed by frustrations are *Called Leaders*. These leaders are inspired by their frustrations into a "holy frustration"— which is a calling of sorts. They are not motivated by self-interest. They are consumed by the need to make a difference. Frustration doesn't derail them because they process the frustrations differently. Unmet expectations create in them energy that drives them towards resolution rather than backwards into more frustration.

In her New York Times bestselling book, *Grit: The Power of Passion and Perseverance,* Angela Duckworth describes these kinds of people. Angela's research sought to find out who succeeds and who doesn't. She conducted research at West Point Military Academy, schools, private companies; and from these very different contexts, concluded that one characteristic was more indicative of success than the rest. The deciding characteristic was a little thing called *grit*.[2]

Grit is the combination of perseverance and passion for long-term goals. It's not about being talented but, rather, being resilient while pursing things you love and feel called to do. Angela used this illustration that fits our definition of a *Called Leader* who she describes as *gritty*:

"Three bricklayers are asked: 'What are you doing?' The first says, 'I am laying bricks.' The second says, 'I am building a church.' And the third says, 'I am building the house of God.' The first bricklayer has a job. The second has a career. The third has a calling."[3]

Called Leaders, like gritty leaders, are more successful in their pursuits. They have a propensity for finishing tasks because they are driven by a sense of calling. They are committed. She adds, "Grit is about working on something you care about so much that you're willing to stay loyal to it...It's doing what you love, but not just falling in love— staying in love."[4] *Called Leaders* are gritty. They refuse to give up because love drives them.

Frustration is Energy

My personal definition of frustration, for the purposes of this book, is *renewable energy for vision*. Frustration is energy. It's neither positive nor negative. It's a force. Power. Any energy source can be constructive or destructive depending on how it is purposed. Fire on your stove helps make great food, while a fire in the forest is destructive. When you feel the discomfort of frustration, see it as an energy to be harnessed and focused or else it can become destructive.

My father-in-law is an electrician. He often talks about the power of electricity. More than likely, the electricity where we live has been generated by Niagara Falls. Now I wouldn't take my smart phone and plug it into the moving rapids of Niagara Falls. To take it a step further, I wouldn't try to plug it into one of the power lines outside my house. It's not the right voltage for my phone. The power needs to be focused and purposed for my phone's capacity. That's how frustration works. It's straight raw energy that must be focused for constructive use.

One of the things you will see on many streets is a metal box near the power lines. It's called a transformer. Transformers (sometimes called "voltage transformers") are devices used in electrical circuits to change the voltage of electricity flowing in the circuit. Transformers can be used to either increase the voltage (called "stepping up") or decrease the voltage ("stepping down"). The purpose of the transformer is to take the electrical energy generated by Niagara Falls, which flows through the power line outside your house, and transform the energy into manageable and purposeful doses for your household to use. If you don't have a transformer doing that, then electricity from the power line could burn your whole street up, or not deliver enough power to do anything.

If frustration is seen as raw energy, neither good nor bad, it must be filtered through a "transformer" of sorts, so that its power has a defined purpose. Many leaders have no filter with their frustrations, which causes either damage or no impact at all. Get this - *the transformer* for frustrations is your calling. When frustration comes, you have to ask yourself, "Am I called to this?" If you are, then get busy creating a constructive strategy. If you aren't, then let it go. It's not your assignment. So much damage has been done in the leadership arena because leaders allow their frustrations to run wild without the constraints and boundaries of their unique calling and purpose.

Chernobyl

When power is unbridled and runs amuck, people, places and things become casualties of its force. This reminds me of the Chernobyl nuclear disaster that occurred April 26, 1986 in Ukraine. The event was the worst accident in the history of nuclear power. The reactors weren't housed in a containment building, so the plant exploded, causing a radioactive fallout that affected Western Soviet Union, Eastern Europe, Scandinavia, the UK, and the Eastern United States. Large areas of Ukraine, Belarus, and Russia were badly contaminated. Hundreds of thousands of people died as a result of the radiation released, and even more had to be relocated because they could no longer live near the site of the accident. It is predicted that thousands more will die due to long-term diseases related to the radiation exposure. This modern catastrophe, where the effects are still being measured today, could have been avoided if there was a "containment building" to keep the radiation enclosed. This is a sober reminder that power and energy must have a containment plan.[5]

Frustration is like that. If you don't contain it by focusing on constructive responses, destruction is sure to follow. You'll hurt yourself. You'll hurt others. You'll hurt the organization. Leaders need to be careful with how they handle frustration. Complaints and unbridled negativity are spiritually equivalent to a leadership "nuclear" explosion, so to speak. Carefully manage your feelings of frustration. Don't underestimate their power and contain them with constructive responses that are focused by your unique calling and purpose.

Hope

Hope is the most important tool in a visionary leader's tool box for managing both frustrations and a clear sense of calling. If a visionary leader gets to a place where they have lost hope, they are in dangerous waters. Hope has energizing powers. It pushes the leader through the frustrations. Hope essentially is frustration turned inside out. Frustration states the problem and hope describes the solution. Frustration is based on the past and the present. Hope is based on the future and what is possible. Hope keeps us believing in spite of the difficulties of present circumstances. Leaders should be hope dealers. Yet, when a leader succumbs to hopelessness the only thing he has left is the negative energy of frustration that paralyzes them - rather than pushing them to success. The word *hope* is derived from the Old English word *hopian* and it literally means to "leap forward with expectation." Hope is a genuine feeling of possibility. It has substance when there is a clear vision and a defined direction. It is more than a wish, an optimistic thought, or faith. Maintaining hope is the ability to evaluate, recover from discouragement, and hold on to the vision of what could be. It is an emotional magnet that keeps people going even in the midst of challenges.

The Bible speaks on the relationship between hope and belief, "*Now faith is confidence in what we hope for and assurance about what we do not see.*"[6] *Faith* and *hope* operate symbiotically. You can't have one without the other. When you lose faith, you also lose hope. When there's no hope, there is no need for faith. Hope is the destination and faith is the vehicle to get there. The visionary leader will get frustrated but has the intangible skill of flipping frustration on its head and turning it into hope. The visionary leader has the uncanny knack of seeing solutions in problems. Essentially, visionary leaders who have "lost hope" is oxymoronic.

A Lesson from *Candy Crush* and *Fortnite*

According to researchers, in dealing with the science of optimism and hope, one's performance is hindered if he believes the goal cannot be reached.[7] he believes the goal can be reached, he'll perform better even if he feels But, if frustrated. The issue is not frustration but hope for a positive outcome. The relationship between hope and performance is the bedrock that makes video games so addictive.[8]

The Psychology of Frustration: Lessons from Fortnite and Candy Crush

Candy Crush and *Fortnite* became some of the most addictive games in history by exploiting a psychological phenomenon that keeps players coming back despite only winning every now and then.[9] The psychological phenomenon that has caused these games to gross hundreds of millions of dollars is "lose by a little, win by a lot."[10] If a player loses the game by a little, they can examine the state of the game, and note they were just one or two moves away from winning. They think, *I'll win for sure next time!*[11] If a player wins the game by a lot, they think *I'm just going to knock out a few more levels while I'm on this hot streak!*

As you can see, video game developers made millions by mastering the psychology of hope. Follow the logic here. The "lose by a little, win by a lot" concept is what motivates people to keep coming back to these highly addictive games. Now you understand the reason people keep coming back even though these games frustrate the heck out of the players (have you ever seen someone play *Candy Crush* or *Fortnite*?)! It's simply because the game is designed to make them BELIEVE they can win at some point. There is a lesson to be learned about the relationship between frustration and hope that cannot be missed here, so let's go deeper.

Video game developers think it's important that a player be faced with a difficult obstacle that they cannot overcome the first time, and maybe not even the second or third time. In order to win, the player would have to really try and try again. Delayed gratification, or frustration, is critical to video game design and popularity. People like a challenge, so developers never make it impossible to win or else people wouldn't buy the game. The game is most attractive when it embeds a healthy dose of frustration and reward.

The same is true with leadership. God programs enough frustration and reward into our life experiences to keep us coming back for more. The key to the addictive nature of "chasing the vision" is in overcoming the obstacles and solving the problems. I'm amazed at how many leaders I meet who are easily frustrated by the smallest inconveniences to their vision. If that's your disposition, you're not ready to be a visionary leader. Visionary leaders *must* have frustrations present. It's the energy that powers a moral compulsion to do something!

Summary Points
- Frustration is a mind-game to be mastered.
- The cycle of frustration is broken with belief.
- There are two kinds of leaders: those who are pushed by frustration and those who are paralyzed by it.
- Frustration is energy, not evil.
- Frustration is focused by having hope.

Questions for Reflection
- Are you paralyzed by frustration or pushed by it?
- How do you manage your frustration?
- Are you hopeful about where you are and what you are called to? Why?

CHAPTER 3

The 7 Sources of Frustration

"To conquer frustration, one must remain intensely focused on the outcome, not the obstacles."
— T. F. Hodge

Now that you know that this frustration thing is not going away, let's analyze why leaders get frustrated. It's important to understand the reasons why leaders get frustrated so that we can identify how to address these frustrations. In my experience, the visionary leader usually bumps into 7 common sources of frustration.

1. Unmet or Unsupported Expectations
2. Resistant People
3. Lack of Vision
4. Criticism
5. Lack of commitment or indifference
6. Restricted access to resources
7. Lack of appreciation

1. Unmet or Unsupported Expectations

Generally, leaders have certain expectations for how things are supposed to go. You have an idea, put that idea in front of a committee, then they execute, right? Righhht. Or maybe, you envision how the revival will go, how a congregation will respond to your sermon, how many parents and kids will attend an event you've worked hard at marketing, when a leader you've mentored doesn't pan out ... and even how a church building project will progress. We even have expectations of ourselves. As you have probably already experienced in your own leadership position, things usually do *not* go as planned.

From your perspective, you "know" what should be happening and what the expectations are. You "know" how things are supposed to pan out; however, when things do not pan out in that specific way, it's easy to get frustrated. Unmet expectations can create a lot of frustration, especially in ministry, because there are so many mitigating factors that can cause things to go in a different direction.

Recommendations

I have three recommendations for dealing with unmet expectations.

1. *Patience.* Learning how to wait is hard for a visionary leader, but it's a skill we must learn so that frustrations don't master us. I heard someone say, "Patience is not the ability to wait, but the ability to keep a good attitude while waiting." Anyone can wait. For many of us waiting is not our choice. How we handle waiting deter-

mines if we are patient or not. When expectations are not met and you have to wait, do it with patience while trusting and believing that God is the originator of the vision and He will bring it to pass.

2. *Persistence.* There are so many leaders with a vision who, at the first sign of opposition or unmet expectations, give up or give in to paralyzing frustration. In my experience, the difference between accomplished leaders and those who aren't is persistence. Everyone has talent. Everyone has a level of smarts. Everyone has a vision and a bright idea, but those who make things happen are those who don't quit. There are those who believe in what they are doing with such passion that they are committed to persist *until* it happens. Many times, God uses the difficulties in order to test our faith. Persistence often shows just how much we believe in what we are doing. Margaret Thatcher, former Prime Minister of England, said "You may have to fight a battle more than once in order to win it." Keep fighting. Be persistent.

3. *Prayerfulness.* The visionary leader's secret weapon is prayer. As a matter of fact, when expectations are met, and things are going well you may feel like you really don't need to pray. It's when things seem out of your control that you start praying. But visionary leaders pray *through* things. Prayer reminds us that we don't have to pull stuff off. Prayer focuses us on God who has the power to change any situation. God's ways are not our ways nor are His thoughts our thoughts. Prayer helps take our focus off of our abilities and refocuses

us on God. The minute something doesn't go as you think it should, know that this is a call to prayer. Ask God what He sees. Ask God what to do. Ask God to give you patience and persistence or ask Him to show you another way.

2. Resistant People

Listen, we could spend a whole chapter on this source of frustration. People, people, people, people, yes, people are truly a source of frustrations for leaders. That is because leadership involves leading people where they ordinarily would not go. No matter who you're leading you will always have a person who is resistant. Take that to the bank.

I believe the whole purpose of being a leader—the reason why you've been sent wherever you are—is to move them—guide them, lead them, push them—further in their journey! And people, bless their hearts, will push when pushed, sit when encouraged to stand and hide when you intend to guide! A fundamental human trait is to resist change.

I need you to put on your big boy and big girl pants right now. If you are a true visionary leader, you have not been sent somewhere to maintain the status quo. Let's get that straight today, ma'am or sir! You have been sent where you are in order to lead people to do stuff that they ordinarily wouldn't do because that's what leadership requires. Leadership brings impact and makes changes. Indeed, you are a leader when people are following you in a certain direction. However, when it's hard to get people to follow the very thing that God called you to lead them to do, they don't want to cooperate. As a result, you become frustrated. You're frustrated with their *resistance and rejection.* You're frustrated by their *lack of vision and their criticism.* You're frustrated with their *lack of commitment or their indifference.* Let's go in on these four types of frustration associated with resistant people.

Your frustration with other individuals' resistance and rejection includes their resistance to change and even their resistance to what the Bible says they should be doing. Think about the business of ministry. We have churches out there where people resist actually doing ministry. They just don't get it. You can preach to them sound biblical sermons describing the mission of the church and they will still resist. You can carefully explain how this vision will improve their situation and they will still fight you. This hurts.

It's beyond frustrating to see dying churches and ministries who fight against their own survival because they fear change. I believe there are some people who have been called to resist and reject the vision. There is a funny story I heard that illustrates this point.

The Story of the Visionary Pastor

The pastor of a church decided that God was calling the church to a new vision. So, at the deacons' meeting, he presented the new vision with as much conviction and passion as he could muster. When he finished, the deacon chairman called for a vote. All 12 deacons voted against the new vision, with only the pastor voting for it.

"Well pastor, it looks like you'll have to rethink your vision," the deacon chairman said. "Would you like to close the meeting in prayer?"

The pastor raised his hands to heaven and prayed, "Lord! Please show these people that it's not MY vision but it's YOUR vision!"

At that very moment, the clouds darkened, and a bolt of lightning shot through the window, splitting the table in two. The deacons were all knocked out of their chairs as the pastor remained standing, untouched.

As the deacons dusted themselves off, the chairman said, "Well, that's twelve votes to two now."

There will always be stubborn, hardheaded, stiff-necked resistance to a move of God. But you have to see resistance as strength-building versus life-taking. When I go to the gym to lift weights, the more resistance I put on the weight bar the more opportunity I have to increase my strength. How silly would it look if I went to the gym and avoided all resistance? The resistance gets me the results I'm looking for. In the same manner, we must reframe resistance and rejection from annoyance to advantage. It strengthens our resolve and our spiritual muscles.

Recommendations

Here are two recommendations about how to deal with resistant people.

1. *Meet with them one on one.* This is not necessarily common sense to most leaders. Many frustrated leaders don't want to meet with a person who has been a constant thorn in their flesh. We would rather avoid dealing with them and find a work around; but this is a mistake. Supporters have not made me a better leader, resisters

have. Resisters have helped me be a better communicator and listener who is more organized, thoughtful and introspective. You cannot avoid them, and neither should you. You have to meet with them one on one. The purpose of this is not to convince them or win them over, per se, but to hear them out. I once pastored a church where there was a member who was against everything I tried to do. I started taking it personally and getting beyond frustrated. An old, wise preacher finally told me to go to their home and talk honestly and openly about their concerns, and just listen. By the time I finished with them (3 hours later), I realized they weren't pushing back against me, but what I represented. This person was looking for stability at church because there wasn't any at home in their marriage. This person poured their heart out to me, not about my plans, but about their problems at home. Just listening to them helped me understand who I was dealing with. I saw them as a person and not just a problem. This greatly assisted me in winning them over and they went on to become one of my biggest supporters. This would not have happened if I did not make the 3-hour investment of meeting with them one on one. Those 3 hours saved me years of fighting.
2. *Listen to people but don't try to be liked by people.* For many of us this is hard. We want to be liked, well thought of and respected, but the truth is there are some folks who, no matter what you do, will neither like you, think well of you, nor respect you. Your job is to be a leader who leads with integrity, communicates well, stands on principle

and allows God to handle how people think about you. Leadership is not a popularity contest, especially for visionary leaders who are called to provoke change. Be a good listener. Don't be stubborn. Be amenable to make adjustments and changes, but don't fall for the approval ratings trap. I am naturally a people pleaser and desire to be liked, but this has not worked well for me in leadership. I've learned that being liked is not the goal. The goal is not being respected. The goal is the accomplishment of the vision. This is not an excuse to be discourteous, intolerant, narcissistic and incorrigible. There are some folks on the other end of the spectrum who don't care about people at all and see them as a means to an end. These leaders use people to accomplish the vision and they argue that the ends justify the means. This is poor leadership. It misses the point of accomplishing a vision together. Both the people pleaser and the by-any-means- necessary leader are self-focused. They both forget the vision is not about them, but about God. God has a way of humbling both kinds of leaders to teach them that it is not about being liked and it's also not about *not* caring about people.

3. Lack of Vision

Your frustration with other individuals' lack of vision, is because you see the bigger picture, while they cannot. Sometimes people don't see the vision because they don't care to see it—they literally choose not to. Other times, people don't see the vision because they just can't. Oftentimes, these individuals, due to their experiences in life or the way that they think, are not able to see the powerful vision that God has given you. You, a visionary leader, see God moving mountains and making ways out of no way.

You see the building of His kingdom in a mighty way—you have a vision of the greatness and you see where God is leading. However, because of their minimal faith (or even lack of faith), some people's vision is very limited. Simply put, their capacity doesn't match yours. This can cause frustration for you as their leader.

Recommendation

Be a good teacher. I've come to the conclusion that no one hardly ever sees the vision as clearly as you do, except for God. Your spouse doesn't see it. Your team doesn't see it. Your organization doesn't see it. Your church doesn't see it. But isn't that the point? Your goal as the visionary leader is to help them clearly see it. They may get a glimpse of it, or may even like what they hear, but them seeing it the way God gave it to you requires you learning how to teach and communicate the vision. Getting mad at people who don't see the vision as clearly as you do is like a kindergarten teacher pouting because her students can't read on a fifth-grade level when they enroll in her class. The job of the teacher is to teach them to read. The job of the leader is to help people see the vision. Many of us are frustrated with people who have "no vision" because we poorly communicated it. As a visionary leader, you must know your role. You are a communicator and educator of the vision. I talk to so many leaders who get mad with people who "lack vision" but the reality is, the leader lacks the communication skills necessary for helping them to see it.

If you have people who lack vision, spend time finding ways to educate, illustrate and paint the picture.

4. Criticism

It is amazing how tiny seeds of criticism can impact a visionary. Oftentimes, when you are criticized as a church leader, it seems like everybody is against you. It's like when I would preach, and 100 people would say, "Good Word, pastor" and one person emails their criticism. I then become consumed with the email and not the 100 affirmations. Criticism has that kind of power over us. That is certainly one thing I notice when I reflect on my own pastoral experiences. Sadly, though, criticism has a way of standing out way more than affirmation does. And the criticism from the few is indeed a source of frustration for the visionary leader.

Recommendation

Don't take yourself too seriously. You're not above criticism because you realize that you can always improve. There is no need in dwelling on your shortcomings because you already know that you are a work in progress. The truth is, we are generally worse than what the criticism says in some areas and better in others. Whatever your critics say about you should be put into two categories: 1) Is it helpful? 2) Is it hurtful? It can't be both. If it's helpful, it's not hurtful. Because if it's helpful, it's not going to hurt you, but help you in the long run. If it's hurtful, then discard it. It was meant to be injurious to you. You will have to use honest judgment and even the counsel of others to tell the difference between helpful and hurtful criticism. I will often ask my wife, or my team, or close friends about criticism because I know they love me, and I will get an honest assessment. Once you get that, you can decide where to put it and move on.

5. Lack of Commitment or Indifference

I can't think of anything else that's probably more frustrating to me than when people are uncommitted or indifferent. These are not people who are resistant—they are not going to fight you. They straight up don't even care. You're planning for their salvation or for exponential growth in their lives, and they could not care less. They're not committed. They're not going to show up. They won't come to meetings. They're not going to be a part of the event. You pour out an emphatic word from God and they stare past you. You can't get anything out of them, and it's likely that you want more for them than they want for themselves. Oh, and that is so frustrating!

Recommendation

Spend very little time and energy on people who suck the life out of you with their lack of commitment and indifference. There are others around you who appreciate what God has given you and you need to spend your time with them. The Bible says we should not cast our pearls before pigs. In other words, don't put things of value before people who don't value it. Remember the seed of the vision falls on different kinds of soil. So, spread it liberally. But when you recognize people who are hungry for what you have, pour into them. Jesus had the crowd, the 12 disciples and He had his close-knit crew of Peter, James and John. But John, the young disciple, got even more because his receptivity level was higher.

6. Restricted Access to Resources

Do you know what it feels like when you don't have what you need in order to do what you need to do? It is so FRUS-TRAT-INGGGG! Can I get a witness? God sends you someplace and He gives you an assignment to do. When you get to the place where God sends you, you are excited because you have a VISION. You *know* that you are about to make that vision a reality. Nobody on the planet could tell you differently. But then ... hold up. You notice that you do not have the resources you need to go forth and do the things. You say to God, "How do You want me to do what You want me to do? I have nothing to do it with!" Indeed, not having resources is frustrating.

Recommendation

The visionary needs more vision. It's easy for visionaries to see the end result. We often see the solution to problems, which I would describe as the "what," but we often struggle to see the "how." This is where resources come in. There are different kinds of resources. I'll discuss two: people resources and financial resources. Often in the context of the church, we prematurely make judgments about what we have, or do so myopically. Sometimes we will say we do not have resources when we just didn't look carefully. In our minds, we have what we think we need or what we needed in the past, which causes us to miss new resource opportunities. For example, I used to think that I wanted an all young adult church. Then I began to pastor a church that wasn't like that at all. I then realized that what I really wanted and needed was a certain kind of mindset, not an age group. I found out that some of the most innovative people were in their 70's and some of the most closed minded were in their 30's. It just depends on the mindset of the person. I would have missed out on great people resources if I only looked for a certain kind of person. As it pertains to money, I could only see what I *thought* my church had, since I was in the middle of a multi-million dollar building project, but God and others opened my mind to givers who believed in the vision who were not members of my church. If God calls you somewhere, He will supply everything you need to accomplish His vision. You just need to enlarge *yours* before you can enlarge *theirs*.

7. Lack of Appreciation

Feeling appreciated is very important, especially when you are working hard and when you put your whole life, soul and finances into what you are doing. For example, I am a feeler: so many times, when I preach, I cry. Yes, I'm that guy. I just *love* people, and I'm sincere in what I do. Yeah, I can be SINCERELY WRONG, but I am not shady. If you are a sincere person like me, you are probably also easily wounded and hurt. You also know that sometimes it's easy for you to feel frustrated in situations where you feel under appreciated.

Recommendation

Get over yourself. Yeah that's my advice. Appreciation is nice, but not required to do what you have to do. Think of Jesus. He had the best vision and ministry ever, but not a lot of appreciation. Even those closest to Him didn't really appreciate Him until after He was gone. Appreciation is nice to have, but it doesn't help you do your job any better. The lack of it won't make it any worse. It kills me to hear leaders say things like "after all I've done, they never said thank you" or things like that. We don't seek to accomplish vision for thank you's. It's nice but not necessary. We are human beings. We need affirmation, but we must be careful that this doesn't drive us. God will send the right people to affirm and appreciate your contribution. If He doesn't send them, don't sweat it. Do what you do because you've been called, and love doing it.

Summary Points

- Frustration is caused by unmet expectations, but patience, persistence and prayer help us manage it.
- Frustration is caused by resistant people, but one-on-one conversations and being a good listener can help you to manage resistant people.
- People with a lack of vision can cause frustration, but being a good communicator of the vision can help visionless people see what they couldn't see before.
- Criticism can cause frustration, but focusing on the positive versus the negative can help us navigate through criticism.
- Restricted access to resources can often be a perception and not reality. God always provides for the accomplishment of His vision.
- Lack of appreciation can cause frustration. Appreciation is nice, but not necessary to accomplish the vision.

Questions for Reflection

- Are any of your frustrations with God? Why?
- How do you balance your frustrations with your personal and family life?
- Identify any resistant people in your life. How can you reach out and make a one-on-one connection today?

CHAPTER 4

The System: Lessons From a Football Team & Sandwich War

"To conquer frustration, one must remain intensely focused on the outcome not the obstacles."
— T.F. Hodge

The System

Let's dig a little deeper and more technical. In Chapter 1 we introduced you to the three ways we relate to frustrations from the bestselling book *E-Myth*,[1] which are:

- **Self-directed frustrations** — Self-directed frustrations are those in which you consider yourself to be the major source of the problem and thus blame yourself for it.[2]
- **Outer-directed frustrations** — Outer-directed frustrations are those in which you consider someone or something else to be the source of the problem. You blame someone else or some external condition.[3]

The Frustrated Leader

- **System-directed frustrations** — System-directed frustrations are those in which you can see that your business systems and processes—or lack thereof—are the source of the problem. There's no blame; just a statement of a frustrating condition.[4]

You may have noticed the common denominator is in answering the question, "who is to blame?" Out of the three frustrations, the first and second options have the potential for creating more frustration and fewer solutions. Blaming oneself and others is often the default setting of many ministry leaders. I've discovered that blaming oneself and others is an oversimplification of what's happening in our organizations, and it is quite intellectually lazy.

It leads to personal despondency and produces a negative attitude to those we lead. The author of *E-Myth* makes a profound insight when she says, "The truth is that system-directed frustrations are the only kind you can resolve. And the good news is that self-directed and outer-directed frustrations are actually system-directed frustrations in disguise."[5] The problem with blaming ourselves and others is this: It misses the big picture that organizations and ministries rise and fall based on systems that allow individuals to function within them, either for good or bad. *Systems* is an organizational term like what the word *culture* is to a family. Culture, in family systems, represents unspoken rules, values, traditions, mores and ways of doing things that make any given family unique. Organizations, churches and ministries have systems and culture, as well. They define their reason for existence and identify what really matters. These systems are so ingrained that they affect the behavior of the individual and the entire team.

I'm going to use a sports example of this, so if you aren't a sports fan just indulge the rest of us for a minute. The Super Bowl champion New England Patriots football team, coached by arguably the greatest coach of all time—Bill Belichick—exemplify the power of the system and culture of an organization. Under Coach Belichick, the Patriots have had 16 winning seasons, gone to nine Super Bowls and have won six, which is more than any other franchise in NFL history. Yet, they have achieved this unconventionally. They are not known for having the best players, per se, but the best system. It's called the "Patriot Way." The "Patriot Way" is a term used to describe the impressive levels of winning, accountability and team-first culture in their entire organization since Coach Belichick and quarterback Tom Brady came to the team in 2000. Former Patriots running back Kevin Faulk explained their system like this: "Some people say it's the way Coach Belichick runs the team, preaching accountability and placing a strong emphasis on doing your job. Some say it's our style of play, with Tom Brady as our quarterback. But truthfully, it's neither. The Patriot Way ain't about nothing but winning, man. That's it."[6] In his own way, Faulk seems to be suggesting that there is a level of systemic clarity in the organization that trumps the personalities. Many of us know this to be true because the Patriots experience personnel turnover year after year and the results are still the same: winning. According to the author of *E-Myth,* one of the primary skills of successful leaders is systemic thinking. When you're able to reframe your perceived problems and look at them as system issues, then you can see underlying opportunities hidden in your organization and ministry.

The Chicken Sandwich War

Another example of this recently happened with the battle of the best fried chicken sandwich between Popeyes and Chick-fil-A that almost broke the Internet in 2019. Popeyes decided to challenge Chick-fil-A, the king of chicken sandwiches, by making its own version of a chicken sandwich. I've never seen so much free publicity in my life, with regular people doing video reviews of the two sandwiches on their social media pages. This generated a frenzy for Popeyes' new sandwich. Marketing groups estimated that Popeyes reaped more than $65 million in equivalent media value as a result of the chicken sandwich.[7] However, in a short time, the influential chicken chain sold out of sandwiches and took it off the menu with no timetable as to when it would return. In the meantime, Chick-fil-A is still selling chicken sandwiches, with its lines as long as ever.

In my opinion, Chick-fil-A won this chicken sandwich war handily because they have the systems in place to avoid being overwhelmed by the market's demands. Simply put, they never stopped selling chicken sandwiches. According to polls, Chick-fil-A is still leading in customer satisfaction for the fourth year in a row.[8] Popeyes - not so much. Popeyes stole the spotlight for 15 minutes of fame, but didn't have the systems in place to sustain success in a similar manner. If Popeyes were to look closely at this situation, they would see that Chick-fil-A is corporately driven by values that keep its customers happy, not frustrated. According to their website, Chick-fil-A's corporate purpose is: "To glorify God by being a faithful steward of all that is entrusted to us and to have a positive influence on all who come into contact with Chick-fil-A."[9] Anyone who has ever been to this establishment knows that they don't just value good chicken sandwiches, but top-notch customer service, as well. I think this is a classic example of the difference between one organization who has a value driven system and one that's simply not there yet. Popeyes has a systems problem, which is confirmed by the volume of low reviews across the Web.

Seeing our frustrations through a systemic thought process is more helpful in finding solutions. However, there are many times our systemic issues are the result of character issues in the leader. This creates a culture that hinders our vision. The real takeaway for me is that we first must be willing to accept the truth about why we are frustrated, regardless of the origin. Be willing to accept and face the underlying issues in yourself, others and the system that are the causes of frustration.

I remember pastoring a church where the systems were good and the majority of the members were clear on the vision, but one leader's attitude was causing church- wide frustration that paralyzed our progress. The reason I know this one person was the problem is because when I had the courage to lead them out of leadership, everything in the ministry almost immediately changed. In many cases, the systemic big picture issues can be influenced by a single individual.

If you aren't clear about the frustrations that can act as fuel for your vision, stop here, and take time to seek God for the answer. Clues can be found in the things you think about most often. What thoughts keep you up at night? We're not talking about crying babies or the bills, ya'll. Go deeper. I have adapted *E-Myth's* 6 Steps to Transform Frustration Into Solutions for Business, into *7 Steps to Transform Frustration into Solutions for*

Ministry below. Prayerfully take some time to process your frustrations with this tool before you go to the next chapter.

7 Steps to Transform Frustration into Solutions for Ministry

Think about the tasks, people, and purpose of your ministry. Which situations are causing you the most frustration? Is it your people, your role and responsibilities, or is it the lack of financial consistency? What do you encounter repeatedly that bothers you or causes you stress? Make a list of these things below. Write each one down just as you feel and experience it. Imagine you are telling someone about them.

1. IDENTIFY YOUR FRUSTRATION

Write it down exactly as the frustration feels to you—how you talk about this issue to others.

What's bothering me is...

_____

_____

_____

_____

_____

_____

2. RESTATE YOUR FRUSTRATION SO IT IS SYSTEM-DIRECTED

Identify whether your frustration is system-directed, self-directed or outer-directed. If it's either of the latter, restate your frustration as a system-directed issue.

- **System-directed:** The absence or breakdown of our _____ system is the cause of the frustration.
- **Self-directed:** "I'm the cause of the frustration."
- **Outer-directed:** "Someone or something else is the cause of the frustration."

3. DETERMINE THE UNDERLYING CAUSE

Answer the following questions so you understand the root cause and the impact the frustration has on you and your ministry. The more you identify, the easier it is to create the appropriate system solution.

- How is my frustration specifically impacting the ministry/organization/team/my job?

_____

_____

_____

_____

- What are specific examples of when/where/how this frustration occurs?

_____

The Frustrated Leader

_____

_____

_____

- What results aren't achieved because of this frustration?

_____

_____

_____

- Why is it important to resolve this frustration?

_____

_____

_____

4. QUANTIFY THE IMPACT

Do I really want to fix this frustrating condition, or would I rather live with it?

_____

_____

_____

Is the development of a system to alleviate this frustration a high or low priority?

_____

_____

_____

_____

5. TRANSLATE YOUR FRUSTRATING CONDITION INTO A SYSTEM SOLUTION

(You may identify more than one)
The real problem is the absence of a fully installed

_____

system that will... (list the result[s])

_____

_____

_____

_____

6. DESIGN, TEST AND IMPLEMENT YOUR SYSTEM SOLUTION

Create a plan and set a timeline for 1) testing, 2) training and 3) implementing the new system. Outline the system design elements you'll need.
- Who will be accountable for designing the system?

The Frustrated Leader

_____

_____

_____

- What are the main steps the system will include?

_____

_____

_____

- What operating forms and documents will we need?

_____

_____

_____

- What training will we have to give? And to whom?

_____

_____

_____

- What enforcement policies and procedures will we need?

_____

_____

_____

The System: Lessons From a Football Team & Sandwich War

- How will we position the new system and notify volunteers/staff about it?

_____

_____

_____

- How will we roll out the implementation?

_____

_____

_____

7. CALL A MEETING

Call a meeting with those involved to collaboratively create a system to fix the source of the frustration. Make sure this is not a gripe session, but a prayer-focused and positive working session that is solution and goal oriented.

Summary Points
- There are three kinds of frustrations:
  1) Self-directed; 2) Others-directed; 3) Systems-directed
- Blaming oneself and others is often the default setting of many ministry leaders.
- Systems-directed frustrations are the primary type we should focus on solving.
- Seeing our frustrations through a systemic thought process is more helpful in finding solutions.

- Be willing to thoroughly investigate and accept the truth about why you are frustrated, no matter the origin.

Questions for Reflection
- Out of the three types, what is the origin of your frustration?
- What is the lesson you learned from the Patriots and the Chicken Sandwich War?

CHAPTER 5

7 Key Questions

"To discern what weaknesses and faults separate you from God, you must enter into your own inward ground and then confront yourself."
— Johannes Tauler

As leaders, we have a mandate to stay connected to the underlying reasons for our emotional output. Let's be real. Sometimes the frustration we feel isn't JUST about the vision. We all show up to our God-ordained assignments with some mess. It might be unresolved childhood issues or even anger management problems.

I'm going to get on the bad sides of at least five of you when I say this next part. Painfully, some of your frustration is more closely correlated to poor time management and a lack of organizational skills! These are areas of our lives that require development. In-depth solutions to these common issues are outside of the scope of this book, but they are worth exploring. So, Visionary, I challenge you to ask yourself seven basic questions if you are frustrated.

Ask yourself:

1. How frustrated am I?
2. Is it within my control?
3. Is it my assignment?
4. What's the win for me?
5. How much time am I spending on the win?
6. Am I sharing my frustration with the right people?
7. Am I being courageous?

1. How frustrated am I?

To be an effective leader, you need to have a healthy dose of frustration. In the introduction, we explored how you can't even define yourself as a visionary leader without it! So, your moment of frustration is actually a good thing. That moment of frustration usually keeps you from settling—it keeps you yearning to move forward in God. Reflect on the definition of *a vision*. It is seeing things as they *should* be, not as they *could* be. So, when you look at the areas where you serve as a leader —in your family, ministry and church—you see how it *should* be. This is the reason why you should always have a holy frustration. You'll think: *This is not where God wants us. God wants more out of us. God wants us to do greater. God wants to take us further. God wants to increase us. God wants us to grow faster.*

Sense that holy frustration. Lean into it. Because if you lose that edge, you will become indifferent and apathetic, which will cause you to also become cynical and unproductive. This is why I'm always frustrated! I'm frustrated with the way Black boys are being treated. I'm frustrated with the disproportionate amount of education in our communities. I'm frustrated with our families being broken. I'm frustrated that everybody doesn't have the same opportunities every day. I'm also frustrated that Satan is destroying families and lives. I'm also frustrated that people are on their way to hell. I'm frustrated about that, but I do not have a *mindset* of frustration. I allow myself a *moment*, I experience it, allow it to motivate me into action, and then I release the frustration.

So, when you ask yourself, "How frustrated am I?" Do thorough introspection. Evaluate where you are. Know in your spirit what you are working with.

2. Is it within my control?

Leaders need not be frustrated about things they cannot control. You might "know" this to be true; however, it is much easier said than done! As a pastor, I want everybody to be saved. I want all my members to be filled with the Holy Ghost. I want all members operating in their gifts of the Spirit. I want each member winning hundreds of people to Christ!

I think that's God's will for them. I believe the Word which says they are the head and not the tail—that they are above and not beneath (Deuteronomy 28:13). I believe we should have more than what we currently possess, and I am frustrated about where we are in our ministry. I need you to hear this, though. I may be frustrated, but I also embrace how my friend Ronnie Vanderhorst describes a Christian. He says, I'm just a seed planter. God's responsibility is to bring forth harvest. I cannot change people! I can't make people do anything! I have to recognize what's in my control and what's in God's control.

The Frustrated Leader

I want you to try something today, whenever you have a chance. Make a list. Take a piece of paper and draw a line down the middle of it. I want you to label the right half "My Power" and the left half "God's Power." On the right half of the paper, I want you to write down all of your frustrations that are within your power to change. On the left half of the paper, write down all of your frustrations that only God has the power to change. This task might be freeing for you as you start clarifying the differences between the two types of frustration. See, some of you are frustrated, but without reason. You are frustrated about things and circumstances concerning people that you will never influence or impact. For your own well-being, you have to give some stuff - and most people - over to God.

3. Is it my assignment?

You may feel frustrated within a certain capacity—maybe it could be frustration with the ministry in which you have a leadership position. If you are pastoring a church, you should ask yourself, "Am I doing what You sent me to do?"

Now listen. This question and the answer to it are very important. Sometimes leaders, especially pastors, are with the church because they have lost focus of what God called them to do *in the place where they are, currently.* Let me give you an example of this. One of the conversations the Lord had with me went something like this: The Lord said, "Why are you spending so much time in the areas of bad soil? Why don't you launch out into the deep, and serve where I sent you to serve, which is good soil?" "Well, what's the good soil?" I asked. His reply was, "You spend all of your time around church people. Why are you, as a pastor, not spending more of your time with folks in the community? That is the good soil, which has such a quick return because you are actually ministering to the people to whom I called you to serve."

I'm going to say this to pastors. Please don't take it the wrong way. Understand this: you were called to pastor the church *and* the surrounding community.

The church is a critical part of the community where God sent you. If you've been sent to Dallas, Texas, then you've been called to pastor that *area* in Dallas—including your church. So often, pastors (and church leaders) get caught up with "the saved" and we (yes, I am including myself) don't turn our focus to the community members, whom we were sent to in the first place!

As you reflect on clearly defining your assignment, maybe you will also find that some of your frustration is the result of spending too much time out of your lane. There are other non-pastoral assignments, which stir up a sticky ball of frustration. A lot of leaders are not leading where they are supposed to be leading. Let's get personal.

You might be overseeing the youth, singles ministry, health and temperance department, the family ministry, stewardship department or any other leadership post in the church. Yet, you've been frustrated by church politics. The reality is, church politics only happen in a church! Well guess what, man and woman of God? There are very few politics out here in these streets. Very, very few politics. There's no red tape in feeding the hungry, in clothing the naked, in praying for people, and in visiting those that are in prison. Essentially, a lot of our church political frustration is unnecessary.

So, take your fight out into the streets. Stop complaining about your church board, committee members, your conference or union leaders, and for goodness' sake, stop church hopping because a church won't let you serve how you want to serve! Nobody can stop you from touching the people God sent you to reach.

So, if I ask youth ministry leaders: Do you feel like you've been called to exclusively minister to the kids at your church? Your answer should be a loud, resounding, "NO!" The same can be said of the leaders of men's and women's ministries. Are you picking up what I'm putting down?

Oftentimes, our frustration is based on the fact that God told us to go and make disciples of all nations, yet we're not doing that because we're spending all of our time with other Christians. We're sitting pretty in Jerusalem. I declare that it's time for us to come out of Jerusalem!

4. What's the win for me?

After you have truly thought about how frustrated you are, whether or not the frustration is within your control, and whether or not the frustration is your assignment, you should ask yourself, "What's the win for me?" When you seek the honest answer to that question, it will help you admit your true goal.

Now some people don't even realize that they're frustrated about not "winning." In fact, I will go so far as to say that their frustration is rooted in the fact that they are aiming at the wrong target. Let me give you an example.

If you are a leader, ask yourself this question: "What is the goal of my assignment?" Your answer to that question reveals a lot about your focus. For instance, if your answer revolves around self, your aim is to get everybody to like you or to get full cooperation without anyone challenging your ideas. Maybe your secret goal is to be better than another leader, or to have people think that you are a better preacher/ teacher than the preacher/teacher at another church in the city. If any of this is true for you, then we have an issue.

Your goal for the assignment should not be about *you* and it should not be about how you stack up to someone else. Follow the same concept that we teach our children —don't compare yourself to others because God made you uniquely you, and He has a specific plan for your life. Another person should never be your measuring stick, which is why, as a leader, you should not engage in unhealthy comparisons.

Admittedly, from our human perspectives, the "win", the goal, the measure of success, is based upon a comparison to other people. I'm going to be transparent. I struggle with professional jealousy. Because I'm honest, I admit that sometimes I see somebody else doing something that I want to do, and I feel jealous. Let me be even more transparent—I won't say anything to the person about it. As a matter of fact, publicly, I'll say something like, "Praise God. I just thank God for what God is doing for him [her]." Inwardly, though, I'm feeling like, "Man, I'm not winning, and they are. I'm not successful, but they are. They're making it happen, and I'm not. See what my friend is doing in his church? See what they're doing in their ministry?"

I don't know about the rest of you, but YES, I have that issue! However, you cannot compare yourself to other people without being in a *mindset* of frustration (again, in addition to those of you who can relate, I'm also talking to myself!). I've learned that you have to keep your head up and keep that jealousy out. Cast out that "hating spirit" and tell that "woe-is-me spirit" to kick rocks! Take time now to clarify this: what is the win for you? What is success for you? How you define success will probably never be the way someone else defines it. God has your own "win" in mind, and you must keep the vision alive through worship.

Write down the goal of your ministry. Yes, stop reading and get some paper out (you should have already had paper out, mind you). Write it down and focus on the pursuit of *that* goal.

5. How much time am I spending on the win?

One reason why many of us are frustrated is because we are spending so much time on things that we're not really supposed to be doing or on things that really do not have an immediate value to our success. In fact, oftentimes we are distracted from what we are supposed to be doing by people who ask us to help them with what they are supposed to be doing. You should spend the majority of your time doing what you were called to do, not what "they" want you to do. I know you "know" this, but I am going to say it anyway: sometimes you have to kindly say, "no."

I often hear pastors complain: "I'm just so tired of this church. I'm just so tired, man. Those folks don't want to do nothing." On and on they lament, "The church doesn't support me ...They don't give me any money ..."

If this is your complaint, stop talking like that. Instead, consider what you are doing with your time. How strategic are you with your time, and are you putting effort and energy into the things that matter? You see, you can become frustrated if you waste too much time in areas that don't matter, especially when you are interacting with negative people. Empower yourself!

- You don't *have* to fuss and fight with people. It's your choice. You don't *have* to be stopped by politics. It's your choice.
- You don't have to get caught up in drama. It's your choice.
- You can choose to organize your schedule and your time around the things that matter.

In the past, I used to sit up and complain about what *didn't* happen. Now, I use my time to pour into the lives of other leaders. That is a part of my ministry. When I am training leaders, I feel good. I'm in my element and I feel like I have accomplished something, even if I only reach two people. Do you know why? It is because I'm spending time on my win—I have been created to raise up leaders. That's what God called me to do. I am here to raise up leaders—to make disciples—and when I do so, I am fulfilling my assignment. I feel good because I'm obedient. Hence, it doesn't matter if every single person likes what I'm doing or not.

You also want to consider this question: Are you willing to work with *the willing*? Many leaders are so frustrated due to spending the majority of time and energy on people who aren't willing to work. If that is your situation, you have a choice! Spend your time with the willing. Jesus gave us a prime example of this. He had the 12 disciples, but He spent the majority of His time with the three: Peter, James, and John.

The Frustrated Leader

Who are your "three"? Who are the three people that you can pour into and get some wins with? If you don't have them, find three people. Just three. Stop complaining that *everybody's* not coming out to your program. If you are leading a ministry in a church, go find a core group. Jesus had less members than most pastors do. In fact, Jesus had less people supporting His ministry than many lay ministry leaders do. He had 12 people, but *really* He had just three. If you want the hard truth, He really only had one—John. How do we know that? Because when He was hanging on the cross, to whom did He give His mother? Yup.

Jesus poured the majority of His time into good, willing soil. And just like Jesus, you have to work with *the willing*.

6. Do I share my frustration with the right people?

Before you answer that question, ask yourself, "Do I have a support system, or am I internalizing all of my frustrations?" Indeed, we all need a support system and a safe space to voice our concerns. One of the reasons (of many) I have not quit the ministry is because I have a band of brothers that I call about everything. We pray together, and we have honest communication. In fact, the group of people in my support system do not take my crap. They don't let me bellyache and whine. Nor do they let me be thin- skinned. They talk straight to me and tell me the whole truth. They pray into my life and encourage me. *You* need that—you need to be able to share your frustrations, but with the right people.

Many leaders don't want to share frustrations with others because they don't trust people. However, it is therapeutic to open up to people. God knows you need to talk things out, and

He has provided people in the body of Christ that you can share your frustration with. There are people who will keep your conversations confidential and who will encourage you and tell the truth. Once you have your support system, you must be open to constructive criticism.

Be honest. Do you keep your frustration bottled up inside because you are scared about something somebody is going to say? Are you afraid to hear the truth? When you do not want to share because a person is going to verbalize the truth, you already know what (or what not) to do. Sometimes you just *need* confirmation from someone else.

Finally, you need to confront the frustration. There have been times in my ministry when I have been upset and my frustration has come out in my leadership approach. It has even come out in my preaching. One day I was preaching before hundreds of people. Little did they know I was frustrated with three of them. So, I had the nerve to stand up there and get ugly. Right from the pulpit. I'm ashamed to say that, yes, my entire sermon became a platform for addressing my frustration with three people. I'm glad those days are behind me!

I had to learn how to privately address people with whom I was frustrated. Taking it out on the entire congregation definitely was not okay! I encourage you to have one-on- one conversations with those people who frustrate you. Pastor, if you feel like an elder should be more supportive and more committed, why don't you just go and share it with him? Pray about it. Stop taking your stuff out on everybody else. Stop assuming that everyone is trying to stop or block you. Follow the Word of God. If one-on-one doesn't work, take somebody else with you. Follow those steps before you surrender to a *mindset* instead of a *moment* of frustration.

7. Am I being courageous?

One of the reasons many of us are frustrated is because there is stuff God told us to do, but we are scared to do it. So, we haven't done it. If that is your situation, recognize that your frustration is with *yourself*. You are not frustrated with God or other people. So how do you eliminate frustration directed against yourself? Step out and do what you know you should do, even though you are scared.

In a commencement address, Denzel Washington once encouraged the graduating class to "fail big," because failure is a step to success. Imagine how many ministry opportunities we miss because of our fear of failure! If the Lord gave you a crazy idea and you are fearing the possibility of failure, just try it anyway! Unless you try it, you will only imagine what *could* happen and you miss the testimony of what *did* happen.

Here's a quick tip, especially if you are a pastor or a leader. If you have a ridiculous idea and you know there will probably be pushback on it (which is going to make you frustrated), simply say, "Look, I want to pilot something. I want to try something. I've got this crazy idea." So, step one, admit it's crazy. Then add, "Now, if it doesn't work, we'll do something else. Let's try it for now, though, and see what happens. Let's just give it a chance. If God is in it, it will prosper. If He's not, it will fail." Step two is to put the burden of success or failure on God. You hope they trust that you are hearing from Him before you move, right? Help activate their faith.

When our church wanted to move to two services, I was not sure it was a good idea because our church wasn't very full. However, I read in a book somewhere that you don't start a second service because you're full. You start a second service because you want to reach a different population. So, we tried it, and we've been doing two services ever since.

Many of our frustrations are due to the fact that we have all these things inside of us that God told us to do, but we haven't done it because we have not yet surrendered to the will of Christ. Instead, we've surrendered to fear. We need to stand up in the boldness of what God told us to do and lead! We need to stop trying to find ways out of it and around it. Instead, we need to go straight at it.

Visionary, you have been called to do something. God sent you where you are in order to fail at some things and succeed at others. Take the risk!

Stop sitting on your dreams.
Stop sitting on your aspirations.
Stop sitting on your ideas.
Stop sitting on the things that God told you to do.
Fear has no dominion here. Jump out there and just try it.
I implore you to just try it!

Summary Points
- It's important to develop the ability to look inward regarding the source of our frustration.
- Going through this process allows leaders to get to the root of the issue which then hopefully empowers you to

take appropriate action in the direction of your God-given assignment.
- Ask yourself the 7 questions for deeper revelation and reflection.

Questions for Reflection
- How frustrated am I?
- Is it within my control?
- Is it my assignment?
- What's the win for me?
- How much time am I spending on the win?
- Am I sharing my frustration with the right people?
- Am I being courageous?

CHAPTER 6

The Theology of Frustration: You're In Good Company

"Frustration is better than laughter, because a sad face is good for the heart. The heart of the wise is in the house of mourning, but the heart of fools is in the house of pleasure."
- Ecclesiastes 7:3-4 (NIV)

One of the major theological themes of the Bible is suffering. Suffering is as Christian as Christ Himself. It's inextricably connected to the essence of faith and practice. In the Old Testament Israel is enslaved for 400 years and exiled for 70. They were under Roman occupation during the time of Christ and during this time, countless stories are told of tragedy, triumph and more tragedy. Christ's mission was all about suffering and dying. Interestingly, the cross is the universal symbol of Christianity even though the tomb is where victory was secured.

According to scripture, suffering, difficulty, trials and tribulations are the ingredients that create character and spiritual maturity. You can't go very far in the Bible without seeing some reference to the inevitability of, need for, or benefits of going through tough times. This concept is so engrained in the fabric of the Bible that Jesus actually made suffering a criterion for following Him. Jesus said, *"Whoever wants to be my disciple must deny themselves and take up their cross daily and follow me"* (Luke 9:23 NLT).[1] Then the Apostle Paul added to this idea when he said, *"everyone who wants to live a godly life in Christ Jesus will suffer persecution"* (2 Timothy 3:12 NLT).[2] When you live for God you will suffer. Point. Blank. Period.

Bad things will happen to you. Bearing this in mind, it should be expected that while we're experiencing the difficulties of the Christian life, we will also experience frustration. Later in this chapter, we will examine the lives of frustrated individuals in the Bible and how they dealt with it. But to think that Christians don't get frustrated or mad is just not biblical. If God expects us to suffer for Him, then it would be ridiculous for Him not to also expect us to experience high levels of frustration. Ephesians 4:26 says, "don't sin by letting anger control you."[3] Notice the Bible doesn't say "don't be angry;" on the contrary it says when you do get angry, "don't sin." Anger and frustration are a part of the game. However, the Bible does acknowledge that there is a healthy expression of anger and frustration, and an unhealthy expression of it.

Although joy and gladness are active, necessary parts of our lives, that isn't what this book is about. As such, it's important here to double down on my burden to disabuse us of the idea that feelings of frustration or anger are evil and sinful. As a matter of fact, the Bible actually promotes that feelings of frustration are more beneficial to us than feelings of happiness. King Solomon, considered the wisest man who ever lived, dropped this theological bomb in Ecclesiastes 7:3 when he said, *"Frustration is better than laughter, because a sad face is good for the heart."*[4] Read that again. Frustration is better than laughing. Frustration is good for your heart. Frustration is the spiritual nutritional equivalent of eating vegetables verses dessert.

According to Solomon, frustration is not just good for you, but it's better for you than emotions of pleasure. Now I have to admit there are many puzzling things in the Bible, but even more so in the book of Ecclesiastes. Solomon, although wise, also said some counterintuitive (weird) stuff. What in the world was Solomon talking about? What does the Bible mean here? Talk about out-of-the-box thinking! This is a new concept. Feelings of frustration and sorrow are better for you than feelings of happiness and pleasure? That's Bible. The point here is that frustration or "sorrow," as other versions translate it, move us towards wisdom.

The second part of the text says, *"The heart of the wise is in the house of mourning, but the heart of fools is in the house of pleasure."*[5] Meaning, wise people are not always focused on having a good time. Wise people don't run away from feelings of frustration but rather leverage them as an opportunity to reflect, evaluate, and make changes in life. According to this text, there are two forces that drive our behavior: frustration and pleasure. The force that has the potential to add the *most* value in life is frustration. The truth is this: many people are avoiding the frustrations of life with pleasure seeking. Life is not all about things going our way or making us feel good. Life is real, not a fantasy. Moments of frustration are a part of the reality we face. We need to pay more attention to our frustrations. We also need to think and reflect more about what bothers us.

Why? Because frustration is for the wise. Wise people are thinkers and frustration has a way of causing us to do more thinking. Unfortunately, thinking seems to have gone out of style in our fast-paced digital society. We have Google now, so why do we need to think? Not to mention our incessant multitasking. We're on our phone and watching TV with multiple apps open, while video chatting and texting! This generation has been so distracted that reflection and thinking are lost commodities. It's to the place now were the practice of mindfulness is a multi-million-dollar industry that simply teaches people to be present, in the moment, and think.

The Bible is telling us to let our frustrations move us to mindfulness, reflection, introspection and cogitation. When one spends time thinking and reflecting, good things happen. It's healthy and it helps to produce results in our lives.

Frustration is a spiritual gift to those who are serious about improving their lives and the lives of others. If we exclusively had good times, frivolity and pleasures, we won't feel burdened to make things happen. It's a pain of sorts that you don't really want to feel and the only way to relieve it is by taking action. Let's look at some of my favorite Bible characters and how they dealt with frustration.

Frustrated Leaders in the Bible

As I began to study the Word of God, one of the things I realized is that if you are a frustrated leader, you are in good company. Just look at all the leaders in the Bible who were frustrated. The essence of the whole Bible could be described this way: God was frustrated with sin and what it had done to His creation, so He moved heaven and earth in order to do something about it.

We see this frustration played out in the life of Christ. He had moments of frustration. Christ's frustration was often seen in dealing with His own disciples' utter cluelessness about the mission. Remember when Jesus got so frustrated that He had to rebuke Peter? He told Peter to *"Get behind me Satan"* (Matthew 16:23).[6] Or you may remember the time in Matthew 17 when the disciples had failed to heal a boy who was tormented by an evil spirit. Jesus was so frustrated with them He cried out, *"You faithless and corrupt people! How long must I be with you? How long must I put up with you? Bring the boy here to me."*[7] Yikes!

Then in Matthew 21 His frustration turned violent. He literally walked into the temple and started turning over tables and threw folks out because of how they were exploiting the poor.[8] He was also frustrated with the Pharisees and religious leaders just about all of the time. The Pharisees saw themselves as the gatekeepers of the status quo. As the standard for visionary leadership, Jesus came to destroy the status quo. So naturally, there was always tension and frustration when dealing with the Pharisees. In Matthew 23, Jesus goes in on them in a chapter-long diatribe of frustration, calling names and everything.[9] He called them snakes and blind guides because of their spiritual pettiness. Yes, Jesus got mad. Big mad. He was a frustrated leader.

Faithlessness frustrated Him. Callousness and the exploitation of people frustrated Him. Seeing God misrepresented frustrated Him. Church people standing in the way of sinners getting close to Him frustrated Him. Yet Jesus' frustration fueled His mission.

So, if you're a leader and have struggled with the fact that you have frustrations, just know that it is not unspiritual to be frustrated. Remember, the Bible never says, "Don't be mad," it says, *"Be angry and don't sin"* (Ephesians 4:26).[10] Being frustrated does not mean that you lack faith. Being frustrated does not mean that you don't have the Holy Spirit. It simply means that you are human and that you are going through the peaks and valleys of what it means to be a visionary leader. Never assume that a good leader is not frustrated. Never assume that you are somehow doing the wrong thing if you are feeling frustrated. Never assume that successful people do not have frustrations. It is not the truth. The devil is a lie.

Not only was Jesus frustrated, so were many other leaders in the Bible. There are three specific examples of people in the Bible that experienced frustration: Elijah, Paul and Nehemiah.

Elijah

I love me some Elijah. This dude is like a Bible superhero and his superpower was his bold prayer life. This brother had so much swag that he walked past the secret service security detail of the king of Israel. He marched into the king's chambers and told him to his face that there would be no rain for the next 3 years!

King Ahab was an apostate, cowardly king whose pagan wife, Jezebel, influenced him to lead all of Israel away from the worship of the true God in order to worship the pagan fertility god, Baal. Elijah wasn't having any of that and literally shut down Baal's operations. My favorite scene in Elijah's story, happens 3.5 years later when he calls Ahab and all his false prophets to a spiritual duel on top of Mount Carmel.

The Theology of Frustration: You're In Good Company

Elijah, bold as ever, is like "Let's find out whose God is real and whose God is fake so we can settle this matter once and for all." The strategy is legendary. Elijah said, "Whoever's god answers by fire is God. Okay you go first, Ahab." Ahab and his 450 prophets spend all day calling on Baal and nothing happens. Elijah has so much swag that he taunts them while they were cutting themselves and begging Baal to do something.

I can imagine Elijah laying down on a rock laughing and sipping on some lemonade while they are in a frenzied attempt to get a god - who doesn't exist - to actually do something. All day long, they shout, scream, cut themselves and nothing happens. When the false prophets are finally too tired to continue, Elijah gets up cool, calm and collected, sets up his altar and then uses his superpower—prayer. When he prays, miracles follow. He prays before all his haters, "*Answer me, God; O answer me and reveal to this people that you are God, the true God ....*" (1 Kings 18:37 MSG).[11] Then, the Bible says in verse 38, "*Immediately, the fire of God fell ....*"[12] Did you hear that? Elijah prays and *immediately* he sees fire rain down from heaven. I need you to get this! He prays and God immediately answers his prayer. There are many folks out there that claim to be close to God and have power, but Elijah is the real deal. He has a real connection.

I think many of you have seen these religious charlatans. Elijah was bona fide. No fluff. No anointed handkerchiefs. No "sow me a seed and then your miracle will come" mumbo jumbo. He prayed and God answered. He and God were tight. They did things together. What an epic moment of courage, faith and holy boldness. Then, dude takes all 450 of the false prophets of Baal and kills them. Then, while it is pouring down

The Frustrated Leader

rain, he is able to outrun a horse in order to get the message to Ahab that God has defeated Baal. Then look what happens next.

Jezebel gets upset about what Elijah has done and how he has embarrassed her false prophets and then killed them. So, in a fit of demonic rage, she leans over to Ahab and tells him to tell Elijah that he's a dead man. Now you would think Elijah would be unbothered by her threat, given who he is, and what has just happened. You would be justified in assuming that this man of God, with these tried and true superpowers, would have a confident, unwavering holy boldness—because he had *just* prayed, and God *immediately* answered him. Oh, but that's not what happens. Elijah becomes frustrated, and his frustration turns suicidal.

Watch what the Bible says in the God's Word translation: *"Frightened, Elijah fled to save his life. He came to Beersheba in Judah and left his servant there"* (1 Kings 19:3).[12] The next verse says that Elijah then *"traveled through the wilderness for a day. He sat down under a broom plant and wanted to die. 'I've had enough now, LORD,' he said. 'Take my life! I'm no better than my ancestors.'"* Pretty much, Elijah is like, "I quit." Notice, he doesn't say, "Take me away from this assignment." He says, "Take me out of this life."

Now let's keep it all the way real here. We have two choices. Either we can beat up on Elijah's moment of unexplainable frustration or we can be honest and admit that we have been there, too. Have you ever received a blessing from God that made you feel like you would never doubt God again, only to doubt God right after your blessing? I am a witness. Sometimes we are the most susceptible to frustration after something good happens. It's like the blessing can almost be a kind of set up for frustration. We get momentarily intoxicated by the good moment and end up with a hangover when that moment is over. Every one of us is susceptible to falling off the spiritual deep end into the abyss of frustration, just like Elijah. It's real. It happens. Our faith journey is volatile. If it can happen to a giant like Elijah, it can happen to you.

Let's analyze this further. Elijah was frustrated because of unmet expectations. Elijah knew how he thought things were supposed to work out. This is dangerous, especially when you are dealing with God. Many times, God will show us the vision, but not how the vision will come to pass. This requires steadiness and patience. Elijah assumed that once he had that monumental victory on Mount Carmel, Ahab and Jezebel were going to repent and join his team. When that didn't happen, and things didn't work out the way he thought they *should*, his faith had a momentary collapse.

Frustration is created when expectations are not met. This is totally understandable and human, but I want to caution you, as a visionary leader, to be open to God moving in ways that don't fit your expectations. Expectations sometimes are like weather forecasts in Cleveland, Ohio: you can't always trust them.

Yes, leadership can drive you crazy like that sometimes. It can literally push you to the edge of totally giving up. On your toughest days remember Elijah, the prophet who got so frustrated he wanted God to take him out of his misery and let him die. In fact, if you are feeling any inch of frustration right now, know that it comes with the territory. You are a leader and are never alone in that. Now, let's take a look at the Apostle Paul.

Paul

The Apostle Paul was another leader who was frustrated. In this section, I'm specifically talking to pastors and church leaders. The rest of you can skip this section if you want because there is a frustration that pastors and ministers face that is totally unique to them and it's often hard for others to relate. Paul, who is arguably the most influential person in Christianity other than Christ himself, experienced this frustration which is popularly coined, "church hurt." Having pastored for 17 years and being the son of a pastor, I can tell you that I've experienced the frustration of church hurt. It is incredibly frustrating when you are working for the church, pouring yourself out for God's people and making sacrifices for them that often negatively impact your own family (for very little money), only to be attacked by those same people.

There is no pain and frustration like this one. This kind of frustration has literally led to thousands of pastors and leaders quitting and giving up. It has led to ministerial families breaking up and their children leaving the church. Ministry can be a thankless job and an occupational hazard for your health and family life. If you are one of those leaders that feels unappreciated for the work you do, you need to lean in real good right now because Paul feels your pain.

I highly recommend that you read the entire chapter of 2 Corinthians 11. In this passage, Paul is defending his ministry from church folks who are attacking him. The tone is of one who has had enough of his detractors and haters. In the most spiritual way possible, Paul defends and boasts about his credentials in ministry. So, starting at verse 22 to the end of the chapter, in his unique way, Paul uses his sufferings at the hands of church folk as examples for why he is a qualified apostle. He boasts in his beatings, jail time, death threats, brushes with death, getting stoned, shipwrecked, robbed, homelessness, and for being cold and hungry.

He goes on to say, *"I've been constantly on the move. Have been in danger from river, in danger from bandits ... In danger from my fellow Jews"* (verse 25).[13] People that were supposed to be on his team were actually trying to destroy him! Do you feel Paul? It's like he is saying, "I'm being attacked! Lord, I'm doing Your work, and I'm being attacked from every person and in different directions!" "God's people" were trying to kill him. In fact, they left him for dead. He was only alive because God resurrected him. If that wasn't bad enough, church people— who were supposed to have his back— became backstabbers. Paul was going through all of this in his ministry and all at the same time. But out of all those life-threatening experiences Paul says something that every pastor and person in ministry can understand. He says: *"Besides everything else, I face daily the pressure of my concern for all the churches"* (verse 28).[14]

Hold on! Did you catch that? Can we agree that Paul was feeling some kind of way? And rightfully so! He was like, I almost got killed, ya'll. But, there is absolutely no stress or frustration like the stress of being concerned about the church.

Let's look at verse 28 from the God's Word version. Paul says, **"Besides these external matters,"** like getting physically attacked, **"What's worse than that is I have the daily pressure of my anxiety about all of the churches."** [15] Oh, thank you, Paul! Paul feels me!

Let's dive deeper. Paul is saying that the mental and emotional toll that comes with actually caring about the prosperity and success of the church is more stressful and frustrating than being beaten or stoned. You see, a physical beating lasts for a moment but the constant stress of thinking about how to grow God's kingdom can be overwhelming, all-encompassing and all-consuming. It becomes hard to focus on anything else except how to move the church forward.

Caring about the church can take over your mind, your marriage, your health and your sanity. It leads to imbalance and obsession. For example, I remember when my wife gave birth to our first child. She was born on a Friday. I was pastoring and had church the next day. Now any husband in his right mind would realize and recognize that one of the most important moments of his life took place in the birth of his child, which means he should not be thinking about church work. A husband in his right mind would not be in the hospital room working on a sermon but would be enjoying his wife and baby girl. But because of my obsessive "concern for the church," which means I was hardly in my right mind, I left them there to go preach a sermon at church. I cheated my family in preference for the church. I was, as my wife later said to me, "Superman at church, but Clark Kent at home."

Pastors and church leaders, you know exactly what I'm talking about. I was so stressed about the success of my church that I felt my presence was needed there more than with my wife and new baby. Sadly, many of us make these kinds of sacrifices for the church and end up getting attacked by the same people. We continue to neglect our families and health as we go right back to our "concern for the church." What Paul is helping us see is that being concerned about the church has a way of frustrating you to the place where you get consumed with it more than anything else in your life.

I want to warn others to be careful not to allow a concern for the church to consume your ability to lead in other areas of your lives. You are not alone. Leading churches can be very frustrating and taxing. Paul is a witness, and his story reminds us just how much we should appreciate the internal struggles pastors and church leaders go through. Their brains rarely take a rest. Their hearts are always burdened.

Nehemiah

Then there's Nehemiah. I love his journey because it shows how frustration, if managed properly, can produce positive results. Nehemiah is doing his job as the cupbearer for the king of Persia, Artaxerxes. One day he gets a visit from one of his homeboys, Hanani, from his hometown, Judah. Nehemiah asks him how things are going back home, and Hanani tells him all about it. He says, *"Things are not going well for those who returned to the province of Judah. They are in great trouble and disgrace. The wall of Jerusalem has been torn down, and the gates have been destroyed by fire"* (Nehemiah 1:3 NLT).[16] Watch the effect this news has on Nehemiah: *"When I heard this, I sat down and wept. In fact, for days I mourned, fasted, and prayed to the God of heaven"* (Nehemiah 1:4 NLT).[17] Dude totally got frustrated. It became a part of him.

I could see if he just wept and went back to his posh job in the palace serving the king, but this news wasted him. He couldn't think straight. He couldn't go back to normal. He couldn't put it out of his mind. He couldn't sleep peacefully. For many days, he mourned. For many days, he fasted.

According to the biblical chronology, this lasted for four months. His frustration was an indicator that God was calling him to do something about the situation. Then his frustration escalated and became a moral compulsion. Now he *had* to do something about it. So, Nehemiah did what we all should do when we feel this way. He prayed.

This was not a normal prayer. He prayed passionately and asked God to help him persuade his boss, the king, to help fund a vision to rescue his people (See Nehemiah 1- 2).[18]

Notice the sequence:

Step 1: Nehemiah hears bad news about his people.
Step 2: Nehemiah gets frustrated to the point of weeping and mourning.
Step 3: God gives Nehemiah a vision of what should happen next.
Step 4: Nehemiah prays for God to move the king to support and fund the vision.
Step 5: God moves the king to do that and more.

One of the best ways to manage your initial frustrations is to filter them through prayer and fasting. Nehemiah took his feelings of frustration so seriously that he brought them to God in prayer. This is a critical step in dealing with frustration. Prayer helps us take frustration and turn it into a vision. Prayer kind of reminds me of recycling. The purpose of recycling is the action or process of converting waste into reusable material.

That's what prayer does with our problems and frustrations. It takes them and makes them reusable and purposeful.

Prayer transforms problems into a vision. Many people have frustrations but lack a vision because they don't have a prayer life. We often vomit our frustrations onto other people who can't do anything about them instead of giving them to God. Nehemiah's response is a text book way to deal with frustration. Pray. Fast. Pray. Then pray until you get a word from the Lord. Then take action.

Another lesson we learn from Nehemiah is that frustration should drive you to action. It can move you from feeling sorry for yourself towards caring about the plight of others. Nehemiah was not concerned about himself or frustrated because of something concerning him; he was thinking about his people. At this point in the story, Nehemiah risks his coveted career as the king's personal assistant and cupbearer by asking for a leave of absence to go and help his troubled people. God honors those who take their frustrations and transform them into holy causes for the sake of others. *"And because the gracious hand of my God was on me, the king granted my requests. So I went to the governors of Trans-Euphrates and gave them the king's letters. The king had also sent army officers and cavalry with me"* (Nehemiah 2:8-9).[19]

The king gave him what he asked for and added in a security team to serve as an escort. In the end, Nehemiah went from feeling frustration to inspiring a nation to rebuild their walls in a record time of 52 days!

Okay let's synthesize this. When a vision begins to birth in a leader it always looks like a problem to be solved. Visions don't start off positive, they start off negative. There is something wrong that needs to be made right. There is something broken that needs to be fixed. There is a need that must be met. There are people that need to be helped. Visions are initially disguised as problems. Nehemiah saw a problem and felt the pain of that problem although he was not in the direct environment where the problem occurred. There are some things that will affect every leader differently because they don't all have the same vision. God has not called all of us to solve the same problems.

Unfortunately, some people are bothered by the problem and do nothing. Then there are those people like Nehemiah who are frustrated *to* a vision then move into action. Be like Nehemiah!

But there's one more observation about Nehemiah that I want you to see. Watch what Nehemiah says after he prays:

"*11Lord, let your ear be attentive to the prayer of this your servant and to the prayer of your servants who delight in revering your name. Give your servant success today by granting him favor in the presence of this man. I was cupbearer to the king*" (Nehemiah 1:11 NLT).[20]

Did you catch that last statement after the prayer? He said, "I was the cupbearer to the king." The fact that Nehemiah is the cupbearer has a lot of relevance to frustrated leaders. The statement was his way of telling us that he had *proximity* to the king but did not have the power or ability to influence him. He was just a lowly cupbearer. It was his job to taste the king's food and drink before he ate it, to protect the king from poison. That's the job of a cupbearer. He was basically expendable. He had no power or caché, but he had a vision. Nehemiah is telling us not only is the vision revealed through pain and clarified through prayer, but it is given in your assigned place, wherever your place is.

Some folks miss this! They're frustrated about where they are, as if their geographical assignment is somehow limiting their ability to make change! Nehemiah is telling us, God sees where you are, no matter where you are. Your vision is not limited based on your place. I encourage you to operate fully from your pain and your place. Continue to seek God to soften the heart of the "king" in your situation so that, ultimately, He be glorified! Amen.

Summary Points
- Frustration is better than frivolity because it helps you to be introspective about your leadership.
- Being frustrated is not a knock against your spirituality. It is just an indicator of your humanity.
- Many times, our frustration is a result of being frustrated with God not meeting our expectations. Our frustration with God is a call to prayer and communion with Him.
- Church frustration can be all-consuming and never ending. Church leaders need to guard against allowing their ministry frustrations to bleed into their personal and family lives.
- We should strategize and create a plan for our frustrations because frustration is the incubator for a leader's vision.
- God is bigger than your frustration and wants to use it for His glory and the benefit of others.

Questions for Reflection
- Are any of your frustrations with God? Why?
- How do you balance your frustrations with your personal and family life?
- Have you considered that your frustrations could be God's way of creating a vision in your leadership?

CHAPTER 7

Focus: A Lesson from a Bad Piano

"Frustration, although painful at times, is a very positive and essential part of success." — Amy Blaschka

The purpose of this book is to get you to see how you can leverage bouts with frustration to accomplish your vision. Don't get it twisted. Frustration is not fun. It can be very painful and draining. Most people have a hard time overcoming it and since all of us will inevitably deal with it, I want you to have the right mindset towards it. There is a lot of research that reveals the adverse effects of chronic stress and frustration on health, performance and our ability to concentrate and remain focused. Constant, high levels of circulating stress hormones have an inflammatory and detrimental effect on brain cells, suggests psychiatrist Edward Bullmore, who has written about the link between inflammation and depression in his latest book, *The Inflamed Mind*.[1] Depression, along with anxiety, is a known factor in knocking out concentration.[2] I'm not here to dispute those facts and create a novel idea about frustration being the most important ingredient for success, but it can be the catalyst for a powerful vision. The key word that I want you to embrace is *focus*. Ask yourself, has the frustration caused you to refocus or has it caused you to lose your focus? Leaders have to remain focused. When leaders choose to allow frustration to rob them of their focus, they lose their ability to effectively lead. How can you lead when you don't know when you've taken your focus off your destination? Losing focus is not the fault of the frustration, but the fault of the leader. I say this in all humility because we all will lose focus from time to time. I know I have, but we must be resilient to regain and maintain our focus.

Although it is true that staying in a constant state of frustration can impact your ability to concentrate, it is also true that moments of frustration can be effective in causing us to improvise, innovate and become incredibly creative had we not had the frustration. Ted Harford gave a perfect example of this in his TED Talk entitled "How Frustration Can Make Us More Creative." He tells a powerful story that really brings this idea home.

Late in January 1975, a 17-year-old German girl named Vera Brandes walked out onto the stage of the Cologne Opera House. The auditorium was empty. It was lit only by the dim, green glow of the emergency exit sign. This was the most exciting day of Vera's life. She was the youngest concert promoter in Germany, and she had persuaded the Cologne Opera House to host a late-night concert of jazz from the American musician, Keith Jarrett. 1,400 people were coming. And in just a few hours, Jarrett would walk out on the same stage, he'd sit down at the piano and without rehearsal or sheet music, he would begin to play.

But right now, Vera was introducing Keith to the piano in question, and it wasn't going well. Jarrett looked into the instrument a little warily, played a few notes, walked around it, played a few more notes, muttered something to his producer. Then the producer came over to Vera and said … "If you don't get a new piano, Keith can't play."

There'd been a mistake. The opera house had provided the wrong instrument. This one had this harsh, tinny upper register, because all the felt had worn away. The black notes were sticking, the white notes were out of tune, the pedals didn't work and the piano itself was just too small. It wouldn't create the volume that would fill a large space such as the Cologne Opera House.

So Keith Jarrett left. He went and sat outside in his car, leaving Vera Brandes to get on the phone to try to find a replacement piano. Now she got a piano tuner, but she couldn't get a new piano. And so she went outside and stood there in the rain, talking to Keith Jarrett, begging him not to cancel the concert. And he looked out of his car at this bedraggled, rain-drenched German teenager, took pity on her, and said, "Never forget … only for you."

And so a few hours later, Jarrett did indeed step out onto the stage of the opera house, he sat down at the unplayable piano and began. Within moments it became clear that something magical was happening. Jarrett was avoiding those upper registers, he was sticking to the middle tones of the keyboard, which gave the piece a soothing, ambient quality. But also, because the piano was so quiet, he had to set up these rumbling, repetitive riffs in the bass. And he stood up twisting, pounding down on the keys, desperately trying to create enough volume to reach the people in the back row.

Focus: A Lesson from a Bad Piano

It's an electrifying performance. It somehow has this peaceful quality, and at the same time it's full of energy, it's dynamic. And the audience loved it. Audiences continue to love it because the recording of the Köln Concert is the best-selling piano album in history and the best-selling solo jazz album in history.

Keith Jarrett had been handed a mess. He had embraced that mess, and it soared. But let's think for a moment about Jarrett's initial instinct. He didn't want to play. Of course, I think any of us, in any remotely similar situation, would feel the same way, we'd have the same instinct. We don't want to be asked to do good work with bad tools. We don't want to have to overcome unnecessary hurdles. But Jarrett's instinct was wrong, and thank goodness he changed his mind. And I think our instinct is also wrong. I think we need to gain a bit more appreciation for the unexpected advantages of having to cope with a little mess.[3]

This is a great example of what to do with your frustrations. Look for the opportunities rather than the obstacles and then put your heart and soul in what you're doing and leave the results to God. The "magical" moments that visionary leaders want are often connected to "broken piano" situations. Those are the moments when you feel like you don't have what you need, aren't the right person, don't have enough support, don't have enough time or you're feeling like the thing you're trying to accomplish is going to fail. I struggle with these feelings constantly. But we've got to start embracing these feelings of frustrations as "broken piano" moments. We all want the ideal circumstances for amazing things to happen, not realizing that good conditions rarely produce "magical" moments. The road of least resistance almost never produces greatness.

Adam Grant, organizational psychologist and author of the best selling book "Originals," said in an article on nytimes.com that "frustration in the work place actually leads to your next creative breakthrough." Illustrating this point he describes how a frustrated leader helped Pixar create one of its most profitable animated films ever:

In 2000, Pixar was at the top of its game.

"Toy Story" was released five years earlier, and it was the first computer-animated blockbuster on the silver screen. Three years later Pixar debuted "A Bug's Life" to critical acclaim, and 1999's "Toy Story 2" was the biggest animated hit of the year. Concerned about resting on their laurels, the studio's founders, Steve Jobs and Ed Catmull, hired the company's first outside director, Brad Bird, to shake things up. Mr. Bird's most recent film, "Iron Giant," had flopped financially, and when he pitched his idea for a new movie to Pixar, he was told it would never work: It would take 10 years and cost $500 million to animate.

But Mr. Bird persisted. He recruited a band of disgruntled people inside Pixar — misfits whose ideas had been ignored — to work with him. The resulting movie, "The Incredibles," won two Oscars and grossed $631 million worldwide, outdoing all of Pixar's previous successes. (And, for the record, it ended up costing less than $100 million to make.)

We normally avoid frustrated people — we don't want to get dragged down into a cesspool of complaints and cynicism. We see dissatisfied people as curmudgeons who halt progress, or, worse yet, Dementors who suck the joy out of the room. And we have good reason to feel that way: A natural response to frustration is the fight-or-flight response. Disgruntled people often go into "Office Space" mode, choosing to fight by sabotaging the workplace, or flight by doing the bare minimum not to get fired. But there's a third reaction to frustration that we've overlooked: When we're dissatisfied, instead of fight or flight, sometimes we invent.

Frustration is the feeling of being blocked from a goal. Although it sounds like a destructive emotion, it can actually be a source of creative fuel. When we're frustrated, we reject the status quo, question the way things have always been done, and search for new and improved methods.[4]

You're at your creative best when you have something frustrating you. It has been said, necessity is the mother of invention. The driving force behind game changing innovation is need. If we quit or give up too soon because of frustration we are limiting our creative abilities to find innovative solutions to meaningful problems. This is why you have to keep your focus. Remember the goal. It's such a waste of your frustration energy to focus it on failure; rather, use the energy that comes from frustration on being creative. Find a work-around. Collaborate where you're working alone. Use different methods. Think outside the box. Embrace a change of strategy. But don't surrender your focus.

One of the things that bugs me about ineffective leaders is their inability to pivot and adapt. If you're a leader you should not be resistant to change. You should be leading change. Yet so many can only see things being done one way. Often the "one way" is their way. This kind of rigidity suppresses creativity and innovation, and intensifies frustration in the leader and those they're leading. If you don't embrace change and innovation you will fail. That's not a bold statement; that's the truth. The genesis of irrelevance for so many leaders is when they stop adapting and evolving. This attitude will never bring success in accomplishing a vision.

Steve Jobs, legendary founder of Apple Computers, said, "Innovation distinguishes between a leader and a follower." If you're leading and resistant to change, you're not a leader. Visionary leaders should be the last people to fight creative measures and strategies that will help to accomplish the vision. Leaders are vision obsessed and focused. They see the goal and will leverage different ideas and innovative concepts if it will help accomplish the goal. When frustration presents itself, get innovative and creative instead of unimaginative and conservative. It could mean the life or death of the vision God gave you.

Frustration is messy, but God can bring some amazing performances out of a mess. You need to choose to embrace the "mess," and see where God is working. If we believe that God is in control and that all things work together for the good of them who love the Lord (Romans 8:28), then we also must believe that "all things" includes both the good and the bad. Frustration and satisfaction can all work for your good. It can be a catalyst for a masterpiece, the foundation to build something great. Don't lose your focus to feelings of frustration. Use frustration to remain focused.

Summary Points
- Leaders must choose to remain focused during times of frustration.
- Frustration often helps us to be creative and innovative.
- Leaders should be innovators, not unimaginative and resistant to change.

Questions for Reflection
- What creative and innovative ideas can come out of your current frustration?
- What are the "bad piano" experiences in your leadership life right now?
- How do you remain focused when you're frustrated?

Notes

Chapter 1

1. Nell Greenfield-Boyce, The Power of Martin Luther King Jr.'s Anger, from https://www.npr.org/sections/codeswitch/2019/02/20/691298594/the-power-of-martin-luther-king-jr-s-anger
2. Psalm 13:1-4 ESV

Chapter 2

1. Dr. DaNella Knight is a clinical psychologist in Huntsville, AL and shared this concept with me over the phone.
2. Angela Duckworth, Grit: The Power of Passion and Perseverance (New York, NY.: Simon & Schuster, Inc., 2016).
3. Ibid.
4. Ibid.
5. https://en.wikipedia.org/wiki/Chernobyl_disaster
6. Hebrews 11:1 NIV
7. Exploring the Role of Hope in Job Performance, https://www.researchgate.net/publication/230219532_Exploring_the_role_of_hope_in_job_performance_Results_from_four_s tudies

8. Albert, Max: How Fortnite Became the Most Addicting Game In History. https://byrslf.co/how-fortnite-became-the-most-addicting-game-in-history-eea671592207
9. Sylvie Tremblay, This is Why *Fortnite* is So Addictive, https://sciencing.com/this-is-why-fortnite-is-so-addictive-13715436.html
10. Adam Nylund and Oskar Landfors, Frustration and its effects on immersion in games: A developer viewpoint on the good and bad aspects of frustration, http://www.diva-portal.org/smash/record.jsf?pid=diva2%3A821653&dswid=302. Excerpt from the Abstract: "Frustration has been present throughout gaming history and is often considered to be negative. However, there's been a lack of significant studies focusing on frustration and how it affects the game experience. This lead us to a qualitative study, based on nine semi-structured interviews with game developers, focusing on the effect of frustration in games. Results indicate that frustration encompass both positive and negative aspects that differ from each other in how they appear in game. Positive frustration is desirable for developers due to it improving the immersion and motivation in games and comes from players learning through frustration whereas negative frustration is undesirable and affects the game experience negatively and comes from aspects, such as technical issues, outside of the players influence..."
11. Ibid.

Chapter 4

1. 6 Steps to Transform Frustration into Solutions, https://www.emyth.com/thank-you/six-steps-to-thinking-systemically-about-frustrations?submissionGuid=4fad dc36- b8f4-4a56-bde8-d690a32d273d
2. Ibid
3. Ibid
4. Ibid
5. Ibid
6. Kevin Faulk, The Patriot Way, https://www.theplayerstribune.com/en-us/articles/kevin-faulk-patriots-way
7. Micheline Maynard, Popeyes Chicken Sandwich, Now A Sell-Out, Is A $65 Million Marketing Win, https://www.forbes.com/sites/michelinemaynard/2019/08/28/the-popeyes-chicken-sandwich-now-sold-out-is-a-65-million-marketing-win/ #7351201379d6.
8. Danny Klein, Study: Chick-fil-A Has the Most Satisfied Customers, https://www.qsrmagazine.com/fast-food/study-chick-fil-has-most-satisfied-customers.
9. https://www.chick-fil-a.com/about/who-we-are

Chapter 6

1. Luke 9:23 NLT
2. 2 Timothy 3:12 NLT
3. Ephesians 4:26 NLT
4. Ecclesiastes 7:3 NIV
5. Ecclesiastes 7:4 NIV
6. Matthew 16:23 NIV

7. Matthew 17:17 NIV
8. Matthew 21ESV
9. Matthew 23 ESV
10. Ephesians 4:26 ESV
11. 1 Kings 18:37-38 MSG
12. 1 Kings 19:3 MSG
13. 2 Corinthians 11:25 ESV
14. 2 Corinthians 11:28 ESV
15. 2 Corinthians 11:28 GW
16. Nehemiah 1:3 NLT
17. Nehemiah 1:4 NLT
18. Read Nehemiah 1 & 2
19. Nehemiah 2:8-9 NLT
20. Nehemiah 1:11 NLT

Chapter 7

1. Edward Bullmore, *The Inflamed Mind*, (New York, NY:. Picardor Publishers, 2018).
2. Harrie Griffey, The Lost Art of Connection, https://www.theguardian.com/lifeandstyle/2018/oct/14/the-lost-art-of-concentration-being-distracted-in-a-digital-world.
3. Tim Harford, "How Frustration Can Make Us More Creative", https://www.ted.com/ talks/tim_harford_how_messy_problems_can_inspire_creativity/transcript?language=en
4. Grant, Adam. Frustrated at Work? That Might Just Lead to Your Next Breakthrough https://www.nytimes.com/2019/03/08/smarter-living/frustrated-at-work-that-might-just-lead-to-your-next-breakthrough.html

About The Author

Dr. MyRon Edmonds is a second generation pastor, community activist and leadership consultant in the Edmonds' family. Dr. Edmonds day job is that of being the proud pastor of the historic Grace Community Seventh-day Adventist Church (formerly Glenville Seventh-day Adventist Church). His pastoral career has spanned eighteen years.

Under Dr. Edmonds visionary and innovative leadership, Grace Community SDA Church has transformed from a traditional church to a community powerhouse, fighting for justice, lifting the oppressed and setting captives free spiritually, physically and financially. Dr. Edmonds believes that the church is not a building but a people on a mission committed to help as many people as possible experience God's grace before Jesus returns. In 2012 God gave him a vision to buy a former K-Mart building in Euclid, OH and build a 7 day a week multi-ministry complex that houses several community outreach ministries for families as well as a 9-12 Leadership and Technology high school purposed to help stop the school to prison pipeline. He believes if you build a school you can close a prison. As a result of this initiative, Grace Community broke ground on this state of the art in November of 2018.

About The Author

Pastor Edmonds is regarded as one of the most fearless, transparent leaders of his generation. He is a highly sought after speaker who travels the world helping to revitalize dying churches, develop leaders and strengthen families.

He has a Masters of Divinity and a Doctorate of Ministry Degree from Andrews Theological Seminary with a concentration in Family Ministries & Discipleship. His dissertation focuses on how to move marginalized black males to spiritual leaders in the home and in the community. He is a devoted husband to his high school sweetheart Dr. Shaneé Edmonds, a dentist, and proud father to his teenage daughter Teylor and teenage son Camden. He is also the author of the nationally acclaimed book, 40 Days to Life Changing Family Worship. He loves sports, reading, cooking and laughing at anything that's funny.

CONNECT WITH MYRON

Email: bookmyrone@gmail.com
Facebook: facebook.com/myron.edmonds
Twitter: twitter.com/itsMyRonlive
Instagram: instagram.com/itsMyRonlive
www.thefrustratedleader.com

OTHER WORK BY MYRON EDMONDS

Made in the USA
Middletown, DE
11 January 2020